JUSTIN POLLARD

Justin Pollard read Archaeology and Anthropology at Cambridge. He is a historical writer and consultant in film and TV. His credits include the films *Elizabeth* and *Atonement* and the BBC TV drama *The Tudors* as well as more than twenty-five documentary series such as Channel Four's *Time Team*. He is a writer and researcher for *QI* and the author of seven books including *The Interesting Bits*.

Also by Justin Pollard

Seven Ages of Britain

Alfred the Great

The Rise and Fall of Alexandria

The Interesting Bits

CHARGE!

The Interesting Bits of Military History

JUSTIN POLLARD

JOHN MURRAY

First published in Great Britain in 2008 by John Murray (Publishers)
An Hachette UK Company

First published in paperback in 2009

1

A CIP catalogue record for this title is available from the British Library

ISBN 978-0-7195-2314-4

Typeset in Sabon MT by Palimpsest Book Production Limited,
Grangemouth, Stirlingshire
Printed and bound by Clays Ltd, St Ives plc

John Murray policy is to use papers that are natural, renewable and recyclable products and made from wood grown in sustainable forests. The logging and manufacturing processes are expected to conform to the environmental regulations of the country of origin.

John Murray (Publishers)
338 Euston Road
London NW1 3BH

www.johnmurray.co.uk

For Steve, Jools, Katie and Freddie

But war's a game, which, were their subjects wise,
Kings would not play at.

William Cowper, *The Task* (1785), bk 5
'The Winter Morning Walk', l. 187

CONTENTS

3 Officers and Gentlemen

4 For Valour

5 Between the Devil and the Deep Blue Sea

14 Unlikely Armour

15 The Great Game

INTRODUCTION

'War is all hell,' as General Sherman was fond of saying and, as one of the originators of 'total war', he did his best to prove it. But war is also very confusing. Long after the event it's easy for historians and old soldiers to write about it as though everything was planned and had purpose, but the simple truth is that a lot of it didn't. War is a very haphazard business and no one involved has anywhere near as much influence over events as they might like to think.

This book is a ramble through the foggier parts of history's battlefields to reveal the hubris, idiocy, panic, and occasional astonishing good luck that actually often lies behind man's most dangerous profession.

This is not to say that soldiers are fools; far from it. Indeed, the smell of cordite and the sound of bullets overhead can undoubtedly concentrate the mind wonderfully. But war is in its nature arbitrary and hence unlike, say, accountancy, it's tricky to be sure exactly what's happening or quite what the result might be. In the stories I have gathered together here, I hope to show just what a bewildering, tragic, yet fascinating subject military history can really be. These are not all stories about cock-ups, nor are they discussions of obtuse tactical decisions. War is not always a mad, chaotic mistake, nor is it a predictable, logical science. What I have tried to do is discover the truth behind a large number of military anecdotes, some familiar, many, I hope, not, and then, rather than simply quote them in old sources, retell them to a new audience to show the full range of baffling experience that is the life of a soldier, sailor or airman.

Only a generation ago such tales would have been familiar to all those who fought in the Second World War but even that memory is now fading and we civilians are increasingly fed a diet of TV-led, laser-guided, 'clinical' war. In truth, war with the luck, lunacy and ludicrousness taken out bears very little resemblance to actuality. Every great general, admiral and air chief marshal has recognised that they can only try to guide events, many of which will remain for ever out of their hands, reliant, as is every command, on a thousand variables that refuse to be controlled. In war every winner is to some degree lucky and every loser unlucky, and both along the way will have fallen prey to a host of imbecilities and irrational foul-ups. It is these ups and downs that are the subject of this book.

I can't guarantee that every story will make you laugh as some are simply too poignant, but equally you won't need a sandpit and a full set of 1:32-scale model soldiers to follow what's happening. I present these accounts to you as they are, and you can laugh at them, cry with them or rail against them as you see fit. But I hope you will enjoy them. Only ink has been spilt in writing them; much more than ink was spilt in making them.

MAY CONTAIN NUTS

No matter what anyone in a tweed jacket might tell you, history is, by definition, a matter of opinion, and these opinions are mine. The stories here have been gathered over nearly two decades from a variety of sources, ranging in accuracy from the contemporary words of those who were actually present to the reminiscences of those who once 'danced with a man who danced with a girl who danced with the Prince of Wales', as it were. Even the eyewitness accounts cannot always be taken at face value as war does funny things to the memory and, at the time, most authors were more worried about keeping their heads on than accurately recording proceedings. Second-hand sources are also vulnerable to the vagaries of fashion, as political and military thinking wanders in and out of vogue. To get to the bottom of each story I have hence tried to trace its source as close as possible to the event recorded, and in many cases to people who were at least there, or claimed to be. You might agree with their perceptions or not, but I hope you will relish their stories while forgiving their occasional flights of fancy. If there is anything here that you know to be wrong, however, I would be pleased if you would let me know.

Justin Pollard
Wyke, 2008

1

Any Excuse

How is the world ruled and how do wars start? Diplomats tell lies to journalists and then believe what they read.

Karl Kraus, *Aphorisms and More Aphorisms* (1909)

What started the Pastry War?

Every war needs a *casus belli* to get it going. It might be a genuine threat, an invasion, or an attack on an ally, all of which seem perfectly reasonable causes. But there are also those occasions when a country would rather like to be at war with somewhere as they have something the other country wants (or vice versa) or some unfinished business left over from the last war, while not really having a jolly good reason to start one. These wars require an excuse. The most famous excuse is probably the War of Jenkins' Ear, allegedly started over the removal of an English captain's auditory organ by an overzealous Spanish customs officer, but actually an excuse for diving into a much larger spat known as the War of the Austrian Succession.

Then there is the Pastry War. The origins of the war lie in the rather chaotic birth of the Mexican republic (see page 25) and, in particular, the ejection from office of the governor of the state of Mexico, Lorenzo de Zavala. He promptly returned with General Santa Anna (of Alamo fame, although he should perhaps be better remembered for introducing chewing gum to North America), reinstated himself and expelled the president. This confusing process led to rioting in Mexico City in which a lot of foreign property was looted or destroyed. However, with Zavala back in power things eventually settled down and the situation returned to normal.

It was ten years later that a French pastry chef called Remontel suddenly remembered that his shop in Mexico City had been looted by Mexican soldiers in the disturbances and he demanded compensation. His claim seemed a little late in the day and was therefore ignored, upon which Remontel appealed to the king of France, Louis Philippe. It just so happened that Mexico had defaulted on some rather large loans made by France, so suspicious souls might see a connection between these events. Certainly France, which had remained on the sidelines in 1828, now suddenly demanded a staggering 600,000 pesos in compensation for their aggrieved national. Considering that the average wage in the city at this point was one peso a day, we can only imagine how much damage Monsieur Remontel was claiming had been done to his pastry shop. Either that or he sold very expensive pastries.

The Mexicans could be forgiven for being rather disconcerted by this, particularly when the French sent an ultimatum, threatening to blockade the country and seize its possessions if the irate pastry chef didn't get his money. Mexico refused to pay, however, and so the French sent a fleet under the command of Captain François Bazoche to blockade the Atlantic coast and capture the town of Veracruz, where most of the Mexican fleet was also seized. In response, Mexico declared war on France and recalled Santa Anna to the fray. Skirmishes in and around the city continued until the British intervened politically. On 9 March 1839, France received a $600,000 indemnity, both nations agreed to grant the other 'favoured trading' status, and the installations seized or destroyed by the French were restored. The exception was the Mexican fleet, which they managed to keep.

Whose first week in the army ended in mutiny, mugging and murder?

There can be few things more frightening than watching an army in a civil war rampaging across its own country. When that army is made up of fervently religious young boys, the spectacle can become truly chilling, as the letters of Nehemiah Wharton describe.

Sergeant Nehemiah Wharton had been an apprentice in a shop on St Swithun's Lane in London, before joining Denzil Holles' regiment on 16 August 1642, and he sent his old master regular bulletins describing the progress of his war. And that progress was a truly extraordinary catalogue of insubordination, violence, plunder, and accidental homicide, all punctuated with pious sermons from Obadiah Sedgwick, their chaplain.

As Nehemiah describes in his letters, his campaign started

with some Catholic baiting, as a group of his friends tracked down a man called Penruddock who, along with his dog, had somehow managed to affront the young soldiers. They responded by pillaging his house in Acton before rounding off the day with the usual bonfire of church fittings (which as Puritans they considered idolatrous), this time including the stained glass from the windows.

The next day brought a sermon from one of the Puritan firebrands, Mr Love, who was travelling with the army, after which the church rails from Chiswick were burnt. The troopers then decided to pillage the houses of Lord Portland and Dr Duck but their commanders rather unsportingly refused to allow this. The response from the men, who had been in the field for only three days now, was mutiny. Sergeant Wharton jovially describes his lieutenant colonel as 'a Goddam blade, and will doubtless hatch in hell, and we all desire that either the Parliament would depose him, or the devil fetch him away quick'.

By the following day the devil still hadn't taken their commander, so the troops busied themselves at Hillingdon, where they were reduced to cutting the church's surplices into handkerchiefs as someone had got to the church rails before them. In the evening they finally made it to Uxbridge where they once more burnt the church rails and then enjoyed a good sermon from another Puritan rabble-rouser, Mr Harding. Saturday brought the happy band to Wendover where again they continued their blitzkrieg campaign against church furniture, but this time they got carried away. Nehemiah says: 'accidentally, one of Captain Francis's men, forgetting he was charged with a bullet, shot a maid through the head, and she immediately died.'

Fortunately the next day was Sunday so the trigger-happy company could console themselves for the lack of action with two 'worthy sermons'. Feeling fortified, the regiment then decided to round off the day by flatly refusing to take orders from their lieutenant colonel and breaking into open mutiny.

So ended Nehemiah Wharton's first week as a soldier.

How did stamps start a war?

The late 1920s saw tensions increasing between the South American countries of Paraguay and Bolivia over an area of land known as the Gran Chaco. Although this area was thinly populated and not, apparently, particularly desirable, for both nations it began to hold an increasing appeal that rapidly grew out of all proportion. For Paraguay, which had lost almost half its territory to Brazil and Argentina in the War of the Triple Alliance, getting hold of the Gran Chaco was a way of retaining just enough land to be called a proper country, whilst Bolivia wanted access to the Atlantic via the Paraguay river, which ran through the region, having lost its only other ocean access (to the Pacific) in the War of the Pacific with Chile. Both countries were on the back foot and neither was prepared to back down – not with the added incentive that there were reports of huge oil reserves in the area.

The war began, quite literally, on paper. Rather than make an official claim to the region, in 1928, Paraguay simply issued a 1.50 peso stamp of their country with the Chaco appended and labelled 'Chaco Paraguayo'. This was followed by a larger, rather more provocative stamp of the Chaco region alone, boldly labelled 'Chaco Paraguayo', with two decorative shields marked 'El Chaco Boreal del Paraguay'. The Bolivian postal service retaliated in 1931 with their own 25 centavos stamp, showing Bolivia with the Chaco appended to it and marked 'Chaco Boliviano'. No sooner was it issued than Bolivia mounted a full military assault on a Paraguayan garrison, at which point Paraguay declared war.

Although with a much smaller population than Bolivia, Paraguay had several distinct advantages. First, it received supplies and intelligence from Argentina. Second, its troops, who adopted guerrilla tactics, could communicate in the local Guaraní language, which the Bolivians couldn't understand. Finally, troops could be easily brought to the region by the Paraguay river, which ran through Paraguay and the Chaco, whereas Bolivian troops had to be marched in from 800 kilometres away. Despite this, the fighting proved bitter and intense, with both sides deploying every new technological advantage they could find, including the first use of tanks and aerial warfare in the Western hemisphere.

By 1934 both sides were financially exhausted and on the verge of bankruptcy. On 27 November that year a group of Bolivian generals seized the president and replaced him. This finally led to a ceasefire in June the following year, by which time 100,000 lives had been lost (mainly to disease rather than fighting), all for the sake of some stamps. A truce was eventually signed in 1938, which ceded three-quarters of the Chaco to Paraguay, although Bolivia did receive its desired piece of river frontage. Paraguay celebrated this triumph in style – by issuing a stamp.

How did a telegram help defeat Germany?

The Zimmermann telegram has to be one of the most peculiar pieces of wartime diplomacy in the history of war – or diplomacy, for that matter. The train of events leading up to the entry of the USA into the First World War began in January 1917 in the form of documents on the desk of Artur Zimmermann, the Foreign Secretary of the German empire.

Zimmermann was tasked, amongst other things, with trying to keep the USA and its enormous industrial might out of the European war, which was then still tearing the continent apart. As part of this Zimmermann had, of course, to think the unthinkable and plan for what Germany would do if the US did declare war. This played on the Foreign Minister's mind somewhat that January, as he knew that Germany was about to resume unrestricted U-boat warfare. The sinking of the liner RMS *Lusitania* in May 1915, in which many Americans had drowned, had threatened more than anything else to turn US public opinion sufficiently against Germany for them to declare war. With raiding beginning again in February, it was clearly time to prepare for that eventuality.

The proposal that Zimmermann came up with was as ingenious

as it was unlikely. He decided to offer Mexico financial and military support, should they agree to attack the USA in an attempt to regain the territories of Texas, New Mexico and Arizona, which they had lost in the Mexican-American War. This, the Germans thought, would keep the US occupied in its own back yard and hence reduce its ability to fight in Europe. It was not perhaps the most carefully thought out of schemes. In the first instance, how was Germany going to supply Mexico when the British and American navies controlled the Atlantic? Second, how was a poor nation like Mexico going to wage war on the largest industrial and military power in the Americas? Finally there was the conundrum of exactly what the Mexican government would do with English-speaking Texas, New Mexico and Arizona if they did get them back.

However, the question had to be asked and so, on 19 January, Zimmermann sent a coded telegram to his ambassador in the USA, with orders that he pass it on to the ambassador in Mexico, who was instructed to ask the Mexican president whether he would accept the proposition. This was the first of Zimmermann's mistakes. The German transatlantic cable had been cut by the British but the USA allowed Germany to use a diplomatic line from Sweden to the US in the hope that, if they kept in contact with Germany, it might shorten the war. What neither Zimmermann nor, indeed, the Americans knew was that the British were tapping the line.

Zimmermann's telegram was intercepted and largely decoded, but this left British intelligence in a tricky situation. Here was the evidence they needed to bring America into the war – an attempt to make Mexico attack the US at Germany's behest – but if they went public the Americans would know that the British were tapping their diplomatic traffic, which was generally considered unsporting. The Germans would also know that their code had been cracked. Fortunately the British had a plan. The telegram had gone via Washington with orders to forward it to Mexico from there. The British guessed that the Germans would use a commercial telegraph company in the US and so a British agent, known as 'Mr H', bribed a telegraph office worker in Mexico City for a copy, which of course he knew they would have.

The message was then shown to the Americans who agreed to put out a cover story that the decoded message had been stolen from the German embassy in Mexico – something the German High Command would consider far more plausible than that their codes had been broken.

Even at this late stage Zimmermann could have saved the day. The proposed alliance between Mexico and Germany seemed so improbable that many in the US simply refused to believe it. It seemed far more likely to them that the British had invented the episode to drag them into the war. The whole story about telegrams and bribing embassy officials seemed fantastical. However, just when even the mainstream US press was getting behind the forgery idea – enormously encouraged by the Mexicans who were, to say the least, embarrassed by all this attention – conclusive evidence for its veracity came forward. Astonishingly this was in the form of an open confession made by Zimmermann on 29 March that the telegram was genuine. On 2 April, President Wilson asked Congress to declare war on Germany.

Which war was fought over a bucket?

There really can be few worse reasons to go to war than over a bucket, but that didn't stop the soldiers of Modena and Bologna from fighting over one for twelve long years.

Of course there were complex political reasons for hostilities between Modena and Bologna but the symbol of the whole miserable business and the rallying call for the 40,000 combatants was a wooden bucket.

Exactly at what stage in the conflict the bucket became central is uncertain. Some sources claim the receptacle was stolen from a public fountain in Bologna by an opportunistic detachment of

Modenese cavalry around 1313 and that the twelve years of war that followed were centred on an attempt to get it back.

Others claim that the seizure of the bucket was in fact the crowning achievement of the victors at the final battle of the war, which was fought outside Zappolino in 1325. That engagement proved a disaster for Bologna, even though their army outnumbered the Modenese by over four to one. Some 2,000 soldiers died in the short, brutal fight, and in the immediate aftermath the bucket is said to have been taken from Bologna as a sign of Modena's complete victory. Why they should choose a wooden bucket as their chief spoil is not so clear, however.

But regardless of when in the early fourteenth century the precious pail was taken from Bologna, its presence in Modena has been a source of civic pride ever since. For nearly 700 years this most unlikely of trophies has rested in the town, its current location being in the communal palace in the Chamber of the Confirmed. A replica also resides in the bell tower of the cathedral.

The bucket was even the inspiration for the city's finest poet, Alessandro Tassoni, whose 1615 satirical poem 'The Rape of the Bucket' (*La secchia rapita*) pokes fun at the inhabitants of the city for fighting over what must be one of the least valuable spoils from any war.

How did a prayerbook start a rebellion?

The pen is, they say, mightier than the sword and so it perhaps is entirely logical that a book can start a rebellion. The introduction of the English language Book of Common Prayer in 1549 seemed to many of the Protestant clergy a very straightforward matter. A new service in the language that ordinary people spoke would replace the incomprehensible and elitist Latin of the old Catholic service. No one would complain.

But they were very wrong. Whilst many in the South-east of England may have welcomed a prayerbook in their own language, that was not the case in the West Country – where, of course, even beyond the confines of the modern county, Cornish was still widely spoken. Reports reached London in early June that there was unrest in Bodmin, and that the trouble was spreading. When the priest at Sampford Courtney in Devon began reading to his congregation from the new prayerbook on 10 June, there were loud protests and he was forced to begin again, this time using the old Latin missal. With tempers flaring, mobs were soon on the streets.

By the beginning of July a 'peasant army' of a kind unseen since the Peasants' Revolt had gathered on the outskirts of Exeter and laid siege to the city. They carried with them the banner of the 'five wounds of Christ', the same symbol that had signalled the Pilgrimage of Grace, the first great rebellion against Henry VIII's Dissolution of the Monasteries. The demands of the rebels give us an insight into the concerns of the people of rural Cornwall and Devon at the time. The ancient ceremonies of the Church were to be restored, the beloved statues of saints which the Protestants had removed were to be brought back and the much hated English prayerbook and bibles recalled. Perhaps more strangely to modern eyes, they demanded that Purgatory be reinstated.

The response of the government was to instruct the nobility and gentry of the counties to order their peasants to return home – a move that would probably have had little effect even if the gentry hadn't been in passive agreement with the rebels. The government's next course of action went to the other extreme. Lord Russell, a major beneficiary of the Dissolution of the Monasteries, was put at the head of an army of mercenaries and, at Fenny Bridges by Clyst Heath on 5 August, these professional troops annihilated the gathered peasants. Most of the rebels were massacred and those who escaped were hunted down and killed.

The worst treatment was reserved for those clergy who had obstinately refused to adopt the new liturgy and had, in the eyes of the government, incited the rebellion. Their leader, the

Cornishman Robert Welshe, was hanged in chains from his own church tower, with the symbols of the old faith – his robes, rosary, and other such 'popyshe trash' – hung about him. There he was left to die of exposure, which he duly did, 'verie patientlie', as one witness put it.

Retribution for the rising was swift and brutal. Sir Anthony Kingston, the Provost Marshal, was sent west with the power to judge, condemn and execute any rebels he found. The savage eagerness with which he took up the commission is still remembered in Devon and Cornwall today. The contemporary historian Richard Carew, although a devout Protestant himself, recorded Kingston's excesses with some distaste, claiming, in one instance, that he 'left his name more memorable than commendable amongst the Bodmin townsmen, for causing the Mayor to erect a gallows before his own door, upon which, after he had feasted Sir Anthony, he himself was hanged'.

It is estimated that, in the initial conflict and the subsequent retribution, the West Country lost more people than it did in both world wars.

Who saved a city playing chess?

Chess is usually thought to be a game derived from war with two sides facing one another across the board and attempting to capture a king, but there is at least one instance in which it may have prevented bloodshed.

According to the late-twelfth-century Muslim historian Abdelwahid al-Marrakushi, in 1078 the Christian king Alfonso VI of Castille and León (known as Alfonso the Brave) was preparing to besiege the Moorish city state of Seville, which was then ruled by Muhammad Ibn Abbad Al Mutamid. Considering that Alfonso had the famous El Cid as his top general, the inhabitants of Seville were understandably nervous until Al Mutamid's prime minister and favourite, the poet Ibn Ammar, came up with a plan.

Knowing Alfonso to be a cultured man, he ordered the construction of a beautiful chessboard and pieces. He then took this to Alfonso's camp where the king, rather than arrest and imprison his enemy, enquired whether Ibn Ammar would care to play a game on it. Ibn Ammar, after modestly claiming to be reasonably good at chess but no more, agreed, suggesting a wager to make the game a shade more interesting. If Alfonso won he could keep the valuable board and pieces, but if he won the king would have to grant him any wish.

As Alfonso wasn't born yesterday, he tried to pin down exactly what this demand might be. Failing to gain any clue and, in the end, dazzled by the workmanship of the chess set, he relented. When the two men sat down to play, Alfonso quickly realised that Ibn Ammar wasn't just 'quite good' but was one of the greatest players of his age. Indeed, it was said that he was never beaten. True to form, Ibn Ammar won the game and Alfonso, in some trepidation, asked what he would demand. To this the prime minister, putting duty before personal gain, said he wished the king to turn away from Seville and spare the city. Alfonso, being a gentleman, was true to his word.

Alfonso seems to have continued to have a soft spot for Moorish culture after that, taking as his mistress the refugee Princess Zaida, Al Mutamid's daughter-in-law. Ibn Ammar went from strength to strength for a time, organising the annexation of Murcia and then persuading his king to make him governor. Having achieved this, he went further and proclaimed himself king but was captured and imprisoned in Seville where his former master personally strangled him.

Who said, 'God will know his own'?

There are few wars more terrifying than religious wars and few of these can match the horrors of the Albigensian Crusade. The Catholic Church in the thirteenth century was becoming increasingly concerned about heresy, particularly that preached by the

Cathars of southern France, apparently with the blessing of the count of the Languedoc, Raymond VI.

Whilst Raymond was almost certainly no heretic himself, he did little to prevent the spread of Catharism, and had several brushes with papal authority. As often as the Church reproached him for invading its land and flouting its rules, he ignored its remonstrances and shunned the legates sent to confront him. Eventually, in 1203, Pope Innocent III, an almost fanatical opponent of heresy, ordered his legate Peter of Castelnau to settle the matter once and for all.

Peter was supported by two further legates including the formidable abbot of Cîteaux, Arnald-Amaury, all of whom enjoyed absolute papal authority. Despite this they made little headway in the Midi. Peter held Raymond responsible, and he was excommunicated for failing in his pledge to eradicate heresy. The pope wrote to Raymond, confirming the sentence in fairly firm terms.

> Do not forget that life and death themselves are in God's hands. God may suddenly strike you down, and his anger deliver you to everlasting torment. Even if you are permitted to live, do not suppose that misfortune cannot reach you. You are not made of iron. You are weak and vulnerable, like other men. Fever, leprosy, paralysis, insanity, incurable disease may all attack you like any other of your kind . . . Are you not ashamed of breaking the oath by which you swore to eradicate heresy from your dominions? . . . Are you already so mad that you think yourself wiser than all the faithful of the universal Church? . . . The hand of the Lord will no longer be stayed. It will stretch forth to crush you, for the anger which you have provoked will not lightly be evaded.

When Peter personally conveyed this message to him, Raymond was, unsurprisingly, a shade angry, but still unaware of where his actions would lead. In Rome, Innocent III decided to eradicate heresy from the Midi by preaching the need for a crusade, for which the usual indulgences were offered in return for military help. Raymond, somewhat taken aback by this, unwisely threatened Peter and, in January 1204, the legate was assassinated by one of the count's officers.

When news of the murder reached Rome, Innocent was in little doubt that it was the work of Raymond. On 14 September, after securing the help of several powerful rulers, Arnald-Amaury launched a crusade.

Raymond begged for forgiveness but the organisation of the crusade was already too far advanced and his pleas fell on deaf ears. Eventually he was forced to hand over his lands to the care of the legates and humble himself for his crimes against the Church. He then made perhaps his only shrewd political move and took the cross himself, joining the crusade and swearing to help and advise the army of God. This effectively protected his dominions whilst turning the wrath of the crusaders against Raymond's greatest adversary, Raymond-Roger Trencavel, viscount of Béziers, who was now seen as the protector of the Cathars.

The crusaders mustered in Lyons in June 1205 and left the city at the beginning of July. As they marched south they were met by Raymond-Roger who pleaded with Arnald-Amaury, offering to place his lands in the Church's care, as Raymond had done. The legate, now determined to see the crusade through, dismissed him from his presence. Raymond-Roger had no option but to throw in his lot with the Cathars and defend his lands as best he could. He fell back to Béziers where he asked the population to defend the city, before returning to Carcassonne.

As the crusaders approached Béziers they sent on a negotiator who demanded the complete surrender of the people of Béziers and the handing over of a list of 200 heretics known to live in the city. If the people either gave up the heretics or passed out of the city themselves, leaving inside only those named, then they and their property would be spared; otherwise they would be at the mercy of the crusaders. Knowing their town to be well defended and expecting reinforcements from Carcassonne, the citizens refused.

Shortly afterwards, a group of citizens on a sortie cut down one of the vanguard crusaders on the bridge. The camp followers, enraged at this, stormed the gates. The citizens had not expected the siege to begin so soon and, panic-stricken, manned the walls. By the time their knights arrived, the gates had almost given way and within three hours the crusaders were masters of Béziers. The frenzied camp followers, who had been told that the inhabitants of the town were the instruments of the devil, ransacked the place, killing all who crossed their path. Knights looted and burnt the houses, looking for booty, whilst the mob dragged women and children from the churches and slaughtered them. The remnants of the population sought sanctuary in the church of the Madeleine where they were massacred. No one came out alive. At the height of the savage frenzy a knight was heard asking Arnald-Amaury how to recognise the heretics. His blood-curdling reply has echoed down the centuries as the motto of the crusade: 'Kill them all; God will recognise his own.'

In reporting to Innocent III on the battle, the legate wrote simply: 'Neither age, nor sex, nor status had been spared.'

What was bad about Good King Richard?

Richard I, known as 'the Lionheart' to his fans, has gone down in popular mythology, if not in history, as a rather nice chap, the saviour of Robin Hood, a noble crusader and the nemesis of his wicked brother King John. Sadly the real Richard was not quite such a charming man to meet.

Richard I greatly relished his role in the Third Crusade but his warmongering excited little comment among his contemporaries, as war was considered both a necessity and a virtue for European rulers of the period, especially if it was directed against non-Christians. What did create scandal, even at the time, was his ruthlessness and the appalling way he treated his prisoners.

That Richard took a rather unnatural interest in the suffering of his enemies can be seen from his behaviour after the fall of Acre.

After a short siege, the Muslim garrison at Acre sued for peace as their defences were no match for the English and French kings' siege engines. So on 12 July 1191 an agreement was reached and the city was surrendered to the crusaders on certain terms. Ralph of Diceto says that Richard specified 'that Saladin would restore the holy cross on a stipulated day and release one and a half thousand Christian captives whom he was holding in chains. Thus the city was surrendered to the two kings on 12 July with all the arms and impedimenta of the Saracens, who saved only their lives.'

The main concern of the crusaders was probably not the return of prisoners of war but the 'holy cross'. This was (reputedly) a fragment of the true cross, which had been seized by Saladin and thus represented in microcosm the reasoning behind the crusade: to return the Christian holy places and relics to the Christians.

There was also the matter of money. Saladin made the first of three ransom payments for the return of the captured garrison on 11 August but Richard refused to accept it, claiming that several noble Christian captives were not included in the deal as previously promised. Richard then cut off communications and, nine days later, on 20 August, took his extraordinary revenge. Ralph of Diceto says, 'But when the agreed day came Saladin did not keep his part of the bargain. In revenge for this about two thousand six hundred Saracens lost their heads, a few of the nobles being spared and put at the kings' mercy weighed down by chains.'

What had actually occurred was the systematic extermination of the entire Saracen garrison. The Saracens were beheaded one at a time until the execution site ran with blood. Dispatching the defenders in this way took a full three days.

All's fair

The most unfair thing about life is the way it ends. I mean, life is tough. It takes up a lot of your time. What do you get at the end of it? A Death! What's that, a bonus?

George Carlin, *Class Clown*, 'Seven Words You Can Never Say on Television' (1972)

Whose side was Agent Zigzag on?

Eddie Chapman was an unlikely war hero, being a professional criminal, yet a series of events put him in a unique position to serve his country.

Chapman had been a member of the notorious 'Jelly Gang' who spent the 1930s cracking safes with the aid of gelignite. By the beginning of 1939, however, the police were well and truly on his tail and he was arrested for blowing the safe of the Edinburgh Co-operative Society. Having been rather foolishly let out on bail, he promptly fled to Jersey in the Channel Islands. Here he was quickly tracked down and arrested again after making his usual exit when attempting to escape from the police – by jumping through the plate-glass window at the front of the Hôtel de la Plage.

Chapman received a two-year sentence to be served on Jersey, which was increased to three years when he tried to escape that September. And it was while languishing in the Jersey jail in July 1940 that events overtook him, as the islands then fell into the hands of Nazi Germany.

Life in a British prison was not much fun for the wealthy safe-cracker who had spent the pre-war years on the fringes of London high society. Under German control conditions got worse still. Ever practical, Chapman decided that his best bet was to offer his services to the German Secret Service (the Abwehr) in return for his release. In October 1940 the Abwehr agreed and he was sent to France for training. To the Germans, Chapman seemed the ideal spy. He was well connected with the British underworld and professed a hatred of the British, which seemed quite reasonable as he was still wanted for so many crimes in Britain. He was also an expert in the use of explosives. A plan was hatched to parachute him into England to sabotage the de Havilland factory, which produced the Mosquito fighter plane.

After a whole year of intensive training Chapman, now known to the Germans as Agent 'Fritzchen' (Little Fritz), was parachuted into a Cambridgeshire field on 16 December 1942. From the moment he landed, the Abwehr's plans began to unravel. First, the British knew about the drop from ULTRA – the Bletchley Park decryption of German military codes, most famously those sent on Enigma machines. Second, Chapman had no intention of working for the Germans and lost no time in handing himself in to the local police. He was quickly removed to the MI5 detention centre in West London known as Camp 020 (Latchmere House). There he was relentlessly interrogated by Lieutenant Colonel Robin Stephens, who was known as 'Tin Eye' for his insistence on always wearing a steel-rimmed monocle (even, some claimed, when in bed). Stephens concluded that, although Chapman might be a crook, he was a true British crook, and he decided to use him as a double agent, giving him the MI5 code name Agent Zigzag.

There now followed one of the great deceptions of the war. Chapman contacted his German handlers and told them he was ready to carry out the sabotage attack on the de Havilland factory in Hertfordshire. In fact the British had recruited stage magician Jasper Maskelyne to prepare an elaborate fake attack, which his team carried out on the night of 29 January 1943. Factory buildings were painted to appear burnt and damaged, fake electrical transformers were made from papier mâché and strewn over a painted 'blast zone', and rubble was scattered over the site. MI5 also planted a story in the *Daily Express* concerning an 'explosion at a factory on the outskirts of London'.

The plan was an astonishing success. German reconnaissance planes photographed the 'destroyed' power plant at the de Havilland factory and the Abwehr were delighted. In March, Chapman made his way back to Nazi territory via neutral Portugal, eventually ending up in a safe house in occupied Norway where he taught espionage to would-be German agents. He was rewarded by the Third Reich with money, a yacht, and the promise of a place on the podium with Hitler at a rally. Chapman's response to this was to offer himself to MI5 for a suicide mission to blow up the Führer, an offer British Intelligence declined.

In 1944 he was once again sent back to England to report to

his German masters on the accuracy of the V1 and V2 weapons then being unleashed on London. His messages – claiming they were landing too far north, combined with a campaign of misinformation in the press – led the Germans to retarget what had, unbeknown to them, been deadly accurate weapons, after which many fell far short of their target. By the end of the war Chapman was in the astonishing position of being a hero to both German and British Intelligence, as well as having German and British girlfriends supported by their respective states. With the cessation of hostilities he abandoned both of them and returned home to marry his childhood sweetheart.

With the truth in the open, Chapman's German handlers were stunned at the deception. One of them, however, remained a lifelong friend so he, at least, clearly forgave his duplicitous agent. MI5 were a little more sanguine, writing of Zigzag: 'The Germans came to love Chapman . . . But although he went cynically through all the forms he did not reciprocate. Chapman loved himself, loved adventure and loved his country, probably in that order.'

What's the best way to cross an enemy bridge?

The taking of the Tabor bridge across the Danube by Napoleon's forces during the Austerlitz campaign is on the one hand a splendid example of how an objective can be achieved without the need for loss of life. On the other hand it is just the sort of dirty rotten trick that really shouldn't be allowed in battle.

By November 1805 it looked as if peace might break out between Austria and France. On the 12th, Count Wrbna, the commander of the Vienna garrison, announced that the bridges over the Danube that separated their forces should not be blown up so as not to prejudice negotiations.

Austria, however, was in a weak bargaining position, with a victorious French army threatening Vienna itself. The decision to leave the bridges intact provided just the opportunity an ambitious marshal of France needed.

That marshal was Joachim-Napoléon Murat, one of Napoleon's finest commanders and, incidentally, his brother-in-law. His forces were lined up against the Tabor bridge at Spitz, which was heavily defended by the Austrian garrison with cannons. It had also been laced with demolition charges ready to blow the old wooden structure to pieces should the French try to take it. Murat had, however, noticed that diplomatic traffic between the opposing nations often travelled over the bridge unhindered and, with news of a potential armistice in the air, he seized the moment.

Several French commanders were sent over the bridge under a flag of truce and made contact with the Austrian troops, asking to speak to their commander, the elderly Karl, Count von Auesperg, who, they said, had asked to see them. The Austrian troops were a little baffled by this and replied that Auesperg was currently not there. Keen to reinforce the idea that the war was over, the French then asked whether he was on his way to the 'meeting', which the bridge commander took to mean the armistice negotiations. He immediately dashed off to find Auesperg and the French were asked to wait, in return for a solemn promise not to destroy the bridge until they had news, as this might breach any armistice that might have already been signed.

It was then that the French unleashed on the unwitting Austrians Marshal Jean Lannes' most terrifying weapon – his tongue. Lannes wandered over among the Austrian cannon, trying to distract the gunnery captain's attention from the French hussars who were creeping through the undergrowth on the opposite bank of the river. This captain was not as gullible as his commanders, however, and, having noticed the movement, he lit his slow match and gave orders to fire. Lannes immediately burst into a torrent of French protestation, seizing and extinguishing the captain's match in the process. The Austrian gunners, whose knowledge of French was poor at the best of times, were utterly confused and didn't fire in case word of the armistice was true, as the wildly gesticulating Frenchman in front of them was suggesting.

At this point Auesperg finally arrived and, with a last flourish,

Lannes demanded that the gunnery captain should be immediately shot for endangering the ceasefire. He then ordered Auesperg to hand over the bridge to the French and prepare for a meeting with Murat to discuss terms. Auesperg was now as bewildered as everyone else and, either believing that there really was an armistice or seeing that, in fact, the French were already in a position to seize the bridge, he surrendered it to them.

How was Santa Anna caught napping?

On 21 April 1836, the Mexican general Antonio López de Santa Anna (see page 3), the self-styled 'Napoleon of the West', was camped on the banks of the San Jacinto river in Texas. He had with him a well-seasoned and largely professional army drilled in traditional volley firing, whilst against him stood the ill-trained volunteers of the breakaway Mexican state of Texas. Putting them out of action and bringing Texas back into the fold should have been a foregone conclusion.

Despite the odds, the Texan general Sam Houston was pressing his superiors to be allowed to attack before more of Santa Anna's men arrived and made the chance of victory even slimmer. And the chances did look slim. The Texan army was concealed in a forest but would have to come out into the open prairie to attack in the face of withering fire from the Mexicans. Nor would all of his 800 men take part in the assault as he hoped to detach his cavalry, under the command of a colonel who only the day before had been a private.

But what Houston did have on his side was General Santa Anna, or rather his eccentric decision making, which could nearly always be relied on to seize defeat from the jaws of victory. Whilst Houston was preparing his men, Santa Anna was enjoying his afternoon siesta. Indeed, so refreshing did he find these little naps that he insisted his whole army have one too, including all the sentries whose duty was to protect his camp and warn of the enemy's approach.

At 3.30 p.m. Santa Anna was rudely awakened. Houston had managed to get men behind his lines and burn the bridge that would otherwise have been their escape route whilst the main army walked unhindered and unnoticed across the plain. Now just a few metres from the Napoleon of the West's proud army, they gave a great shout of 'Remember the Alamo!' and charged, stopping only to fire on the sleepy and bewildered Mexican troops.

A chaotic rout ensued. The Mexicans were unable to assume their usual firing formations and were unused to close-quarter, hand-to-hand fighting. Many simply fled while those that did valiantly try to turn back the Texan tide were mown down. In under twenty minutes, 630 Mexicans were killed and 730 taken prisoner. Santa Anna's contribution to the engagement was short and frankly unhelpful. Waking to the sound of the charge, he shouted, 'The enemy is upon us,' and promptly ran away.

He was found the following day, trying to pass himself off as an ordinary soldier, having discarded his elaborate general's uniform. Unfortunately he had forgotten to remove his silk shirt, which made his captors suspicious. Their suspicions were confirmed when, on his being brought among the other prisoners, they all rose and saluted him as 'El Presidente!' For Santa Anna, the war was over.

Which French general couldn't keep mum?

It is hard enough prosecuting a prolonged and bloody war against a dogged enemy without having to fight your own troops but, thanks to a series of failures, that's exactly what happened to the French forces in 1917.

With the war in Europe apparently stalled in the deadlock of trench warfare, it seemed to the French that some new blood in the command might make a breakthrough. Therefore the well-liked French commander-in-chief Joseph Joffre, known to his men as 'Papa', was replaced on 13 December 1916 by General Robert Nivelle, a man with a scheme to end the war. From sub-lieutenant in 1878, he had risen spectacularly through the ranks to this final promotion over the heads of the army group commanders, which placed him in a position of supreme control where he could put his plan into action.

He was a charismatic figure, suave, confident and popular with his allies thanks to his fluent English, which he had learnt from his English mother. He was also popular with the French prime minister as his plan seemed to offer an end to the deadlock. Put simply, Nivelle believed that the problem on the Western Front had always been that advances were not backed up quickly enough by reserves. He proposed a rolling barrage where the artillery fired and moved forward at the same time, the infantry taking ground in front of them as they drove the shelled Germans ever further back.

It was probably a good idea, given that he had already had great success moving his artillery forward in battle rather than leaving it at the back, pounding the fighting terrain to pieces as so many of his fellow commanders chose to do. And no one thought it a better proposal than Nivelle himself, who told everyone about it. Everyone. This of course proved his great mistake. Nivelle told journalists, soldiers, farmers, anyone and everyone, and so, not surprisingly, his new strategy eventually came to German ears. The French were now deeply compromised as the Germans knew where the attack would take place and could strengthen their defences, which they did. Undeterred, Nivelle launched the attack anyway, in April 1917.

This was his last mistake. Against a heavily reinforced enemy, the attack was a disaster. None of the tanks promised him made it to the front line; the reserves couldn't move forward fast enough as the communication trenches were too narrow; and, under the weight of casualties, the French medical system collapsed, leaving men to die needlessly of their wounds.

By the end of the month, Nivelle had been removed but the damage had been done. The French army mutinied, and a month later about half their fighting force was effectively 'on strike', demanding better food and conditions. Their new commander, Philippe Pétain, had to take drastic action, particularly as news of the Russian revolution was also sweeping through the ranks. In all, 3,427 courts martial were set up, at which 23,383 men were convicted of various forms of mutiny. On the plus side, the troops were now granted better food and the number of men on the front line was reduced.

So the French army went back to work after their Nivelle interlude, much to the relief of the British, ANZAC, Canadian and South African forces who had just fought the Battle of Passchendaele to take the heat off the French lines. Even more fortunate was the news coming from spies in Germany that the German High Command had entirely failed to notice the mutiny and thus hadn't exploited their advantage.

How many men does it take to capture Athens?

On 23 September 1864, Lieutenant General Nathan Bedford Forrest was quietly moving his Confederate force up towards Athens, Alabama. Having cut the telegraph wire and dug up the railroad track, his men encircled the town and trained their artillery on the large fort where Union commander Colonel Wallace Campbell and his 110th United States Colored Infantry were now holed up.

Forrest's approach had been so stealthy that it was only when the main body of his army was in sight that Campbell even noticed he was there. Yet all was not lost for the Union. Forrest's army, according to the pickets sent out to cover their movement, was not large – they estimated around 3,000 strong – Campbell was in a well-defended position, so he determined to make a fight of it.

The thought of a long siege didn't appeal very much to Forrest, however, who, as Campbell's scouts had rightly guessed, did not have as large an army as he would like – and so he tried a little bravura. Sending a messenger between the lines, he demanded the immediate and absolute surrender of Campbell, his men, the town and all its supplies as he had their position completely invested with, he claimed, 8,000 men. He added that if Campbell really insisted on fighting, the inevitable, terrible losses among his own men would be on his head.

This ultimatum was designed to scare Campbell and in that it failed almost completely. The Union colonel wrote back: 'I have the honour to decline your demand of this date.'

This placed Forrest in a tricky position. If he had the men he claimed, he should now attack and prove the overwhelming superiority of his force. If he didn't, Campbell would know that his hunch was right and that the Confederate force was far smaller than claimed – which of course it was.

Still unwilling to get into a firefight where he knew his men could come off badly, Forrest tried one last stratagem. Sending in another note to Campbell, he asked the Union commander to meet him under a flag of truce outside the fort. His adversary agreed. After the two men met and shook hands, Forrest asked Campbell whether he would care to inspect his men. Campbell, keen to get the measure of his enemy, enthusiastically agreed. At this point Forrest's plan went into action. As Campbell moved past each group of soldiers and each artillery piece, they were quickly spirited away from behind him and moved to a new position ahead, so the unsuspecting Union colonel actually found himself inspecting the same men and guns over and over again in different places. After this exhaustive tour, he finally returned to the fort where he announced to his men that he had been wrong: the Confederate army was indeed huge and completely surrounding them. He therefore ordered their immediate and complete surrender.

Why can't you trust the pope's son?

Cesare Borgia was studying at the university in Pisa when his dad, Rodrigo, became Pope Alexander VI in 1492. He immediately returned to Rome and within a fortnight had been created archbishop of Valencia at the tender age of seventeen. The clerical life proved a little dull for Cesare, however, and he coveted the position of his elder brother, John of Gandia, as commander of the papal army. It was scandalously suggested that he also vied with John for the incestuous love of their sister, Lucrezia.

In June 1496, John was brutally murdered and his body dumped in the Tiber. Few, even at the time, doubted that Cesare was responsible. Cesare now took command of the papal army and began to reassert the papal claim over the area of Emilia-Romagna, which was nominally in the pope's control but actually ruled by a group of nobles. To help him, he married Charlotte of Navarre while visiting the French court and eagerly accepted the mercenaries that came as part of the deal. Within a few days he had abandoned his wife and set off for Italy with his true love – her troops. At Capua he allowed his men to pillage the captured city, whilst taking back to Rome forty of the prettiest girls to satisfy the personal requirements of himself and his father.

Although much of Emilia-Romagna quickly fell to him, four nobles held out. Cesare promised to leave them to their own affairs if they supported him in his foreign wars. Gradually the nobles grew to trust Cesare who scrupulously avoided impinging on their jurisdiction. After he had captured Sinigaglia he invited them to the victory celebrations. As soon as they arrived they were seized and strangled.

Pope Alexander VI made Cesare Duke of Romagna and the two strengthened their hold on the country by a series of horrific murders, including that of a duke and an archbishop. Power was not to be Cesare's for long, however. In August 1503 both he and his father fell ill after a banquet – it was believed that they ate poisoned dishes meant for one of their guests. Alexander died but Cesare survived, only to find that during his illness his enemies had removed his men from office and elected an anti-Borgia pope. Cesare fled to his father-in-law's court in Navarre where he gained a command in the army. He was later killed in a skirmish with the Spanish, aged thirty-two.

What was Sun Bin's revenge?

There are many spectacular stories surviving from the Warring States period of Chinese history, which may perhaps be explained by the fact that it is the time at which Sun Tzu was writing the seminal Chinese warcraft manual, *The Art of War*. So it is also appropriate that one of the most brilliant recorded stratagems was instigated by Sun Bin, who was probably one of Sun Tzu's descendants and helped to edit his great work.

In 341 BC, Sun Bin was fighting his old adversary and one-time fellow student, Pang Juan, who, jealous of Sun Bin's military knowledge, had previously arranged to have the poor man's knees mutilated. These two men now led opposing armies in the field, Pang Juan fighting for the state of Wei, and Sun Bin, rather confusingly, fighting for King Wei of the Qi.

Sun Bin, finding himself in a position where a full frontal attack was too risky, decided to use a stratagem against his old foe. He knew that Pang Juan had a very low opinion of the soldiers of Qi, believing them to be cowards, and he decided to exploit this. Knowing that Pang Juan would have scouts out assessing his strength each night, Sun Bin ordered 100,000 camp stoves to be lit. The next night he ordered 50,000 to be lit and the next only 20,000. News, of course, quickly got back to Pang Juan that the Qi army was getting smaller every night and this reinforced the commander's prejudices, convincing him that the enemy were deserting in droves rather than preparing to stand and fight.

The next part of the tale smacks of legend but adds a nice flourish to finish the story. Knowing his enemy was now wildly overconfident, Sun Bin ordered his army to fall back, abandoning equipment as they went to increase the impression of full retreat. Reaching a narrow ravine at Maling, Sun Bin ordered an inscription written on a tree in the middle of the narrow defile. That night Pang Juan and his cavalry stormed up the valley, believing their enemy were routed. On reaching the tree, the commander saw the writing and called for a torch. Holding the light close to the trunk, he read the words, 'Pang Juan shall die in Malingdao, under this tree.' Moments later, as Pang Juan was illuminated by his own torch, Sun Bin's 10,000 hidden archers shot him dead. With their leader gone, the army of Wei panicked and fled.

In fact, historically, Pang Juan wasn't killed, although his elite troops were ambushed, he had indeed been duped and his army was left reeling. In the face of this humiliation he committed suicide. Sun Bin's stratagem was commemorated in Chinese history as 'The Tactic of the Missing Stoves'.

When was throwing dice fatal?

During the English Civil War, Cromwell's own troops could often be as troublesome to him as the king's and never more so than on 15 December 1647 at the first great 'rendezvous' of the New Model Army.

On that day just outside Ware in Hertfordshire, at Corkbush Field, two regiments led by Robert Liburne and Thomas Harrison mutinied. Many of the soldiers were unhappy with the idea that any accommodation could be made with the king and were agitating for the creation of a republic. Some had formalised these thoughts into a political agenda and called themselves 'Levellers'. A contemporary source describes their intention 'to sett all things straight, and rayse a parity and community in the kingdom'.

The Levellers had put together a manifesto, known as 'The Agreement of the People', which many of Liburne and Harrison's troops were wearing in their hats, much to the disgust of Cromwell. He in turn had gathered the army there to ensure that they agreed his own army manifesto, known as 'The Heads of the Proposals'.

Negotiations opened over shouts from the mutineers of 'England's freedom, soldiers' rights', but Thomas Fairfax, the commander-in-chief of Cromwell's New Model Army, soon persuaded Harrison's regiment to sign the 'Heads'. Liburne's men were not so easily swayed, however, and when one of Fairfax's officers approached them they threw stones, wounding him. Incensed, Cromwell rode in among the men, brandishing his sword and ordering them to take the papers from their hats. This bold show seems to have completely overawed the mutineers and they complied, begging Cromwell for mercy.

This now put him, like any leader at the end of a mutiny, in a difficult situation. Whilst there are nearly always casualties in war, it is generally considered poor form to shoot your own troops. There was no point in punishing a whole regiment that was now offering to fight for the cause; indeed, it could simply help the mutiny to spread. Equally, letting the leaders of the Levellers go free could create more problems in the future. In fact, the whole purpose of the rendezvous at Corkbush Field had been to nip this 'levelling' in the bud.

Cromwell's answer was to arrest and try the ringleaders in a hastily convened court martial but then let fate play a role. As they had mutinied in front of a substantial portion of the army, it is hardly surprising that the three identified instigators didn't have a leg to stand on. All were summarily convicted and sentenced to death. However, Cromwell needed to make only one example so he made the three men play a deadly game. Each in turn threw dice to see who would live and who would die. The lowest score fell to Private Richard Arnold. He was shot on the spot.

How did a boy from *Fame* beat the French at their own game?

Many of the smaller acts of heroism in war, particularly those carried out by the lower ranks, can easily go unreported, but thanks to the Annual Register for 1811 at least one such small but telling incident has come down to us.

The hero in question is so lowly that the register, whilst lauding the incident, doesn't consider it necessary to tell us his name. He was just a thirteen-year-old boy aboard the merchant vessel *Fame*, working out of Carron on the Firth of Forth, on a voyage from

London to Arbroath with a cargo of flax and hemp. The North Sea was a more dangerous place than usual in 1811, thanks to a number of French privateers cruising the coast, looking for British ships to capture and take back to France as prizes. At one o'clock in the afternoon of 25 October, that became the fate of the *Fame* as the sixteen-gun privateer *Grand Fury* came alongside and boarded. The *Fame* was an easy target, being unarmed; indeed, the *Grand Fury* had only four of its guns mounted for the 'attack'. Within minutes the crew of the *Fame* were removed and replaced with six Frenchmen who were charged with taking the prize back to France. Of the *Fame*'s crew only an old man and the ship's boy were left aboard as they represented no threat. Or so the French thought.

As night fell a rising northerly gale came on and the little ship with its unfamiliar crew soon became unmanageable. Being driven before the wind, neither the Frenchmen nor the old man had any idea where they were, and the compass was useless as the candles that lit the binnacle were 'missing' – either having burnt down or been thrown overboard. Perhaps the latter was more likely for there was someone on board who not only knew where he was but had a plan. The ship's boy realised that they were being driven into the Firth of Forth when he saw the light on the tiny island of Inch Keith and told his guards that, as he knew the ship's true position, he was the only one who could save them from being wrecked. The Frenchmen reluctantly agreed to give him the helm and he confidently steered straight up the Forth. But if they uttered a sigh of relief at their deliverance, it was to be short-lived. The boy sailed straight past the British warship *Rebecca*, then riding at anchor in St Margaret's Hope, and took the opportunity to shout across in English, which his French captors didn't understand, that he had six prisoners on board and needed assistance. Initially the crew of the *Rebecca* thought it a joke but when he repeated the request they sent out a boat.

As they came aboard the boy grabbed the leading Frenchman's pistols and claimed them as his by right of conquest. No amount of persuading from the crew of the *Rebecca* could make him give them up. The bemused Frenchmen, who were now taken prisoner themselves, had to admit that the boy was an excellent steersman and had saved both their lives and the ship.

With no name given for this young hero, we have no way of knowing whether his future career was as dazzling as this plucky start suggests. Perhaps aware that, as a mere ship's boy, he'd get precious little for his bravery, he held on to the French pistols that might bring him a shilling or two. The Annual Register was more optimistic, however: 'Conduct like this, in a boy of about thirteen years of age, is truly British, and will certainly not be allowed to pass without its due reward.'

Why did Darius keep his army awake?

In many ways Gaugamela was a classic victory for Alexander the Great but it wasn't won simply on the battlefield. For all Alexander's tactical genius (see page 250 for his father's military genius), he also had a great knack for making his opponent do very stupid things, none more so than Darius III, king of Persia.

The run-up to the Battle of Gaugamela didn't look good for Alexander. In the first place he had to march long distances to reach the Persian army, which had decided to wait for him around the town of Gaugamela. The Greek army spent its life on the march and would have to meet their biggest test to date when footsore and tired. The Persian army, on the other hand, would be well rested and eager for battle.

Then there was the sheer size of the challenge. Alexander's army was relatively small, whereas Darius', drawn from all over his huge Achaemenid empire, was enormous: in fact, three times the size of Alexander's. Having arrived at the battle site well in advance, Darius had taken the time to choose his ground and level it for his war chariots and elephants, military innovations that Alexander simply didn't have (but see page 114 for ancient anti-elephant tactics). The Persian army was also much more heavily armoured with five times as many horsemen, so, when Alexander and his weary host were reported to be approaching, the result seemed a foregone conclusion.

But, however heavily weighted the odds are in the favour of one side, there is always the opportunity for their leader to throw it away, which is exactly what Darius did. Alexander's army were fatigued and hungry; Darius' was fresh and fit. An immediate attack seemed the logical step but instead he waited, allowing the Macedonians not one but three days to recover their strength. Each morning Alexander would send forward scouts who would report on the massing of the Persian army. These huge forces would wait in vain all day long for a Macedonian attack before trudging back to camp at nightfall. On the third day Alexander himself reconnoitred before retiring to finalise his battle plan. Then, at the end of the evening's work, he posted pickets around his camp and got a good night's sleep.

Darius, however, did not. He had given Alexander the initiative and had spent three days like an irate passenger at a bus stop, arriving every morning and waiting all day for a bus that never came. But, he thought, perhaps Alexander would attack at night – that would, after all, be a sensible move for a smaller army. It was at this point that Darius made another wrong turn. Having reached the site early, chosen the ground, rested and fed his men – in fact, with everything in his favour – he now kept his army up all night, expecting Alexander to make his move. Alexander was, of course, asleep; indeed, it was reported that his generals had trouble waking him the following morning.

When the two sides finally squared up for battle that day, Alexander had successfully reversed the roles without a single arrow being fired. The Persian army appeared exhausted and drawn, weary from waiting and heavy with sleep. Alexander's army was alert and ready. The result now really was a foregone conclusion. It would be Darius' final defeat. Although he personally escaped the rout, he would be assassinated by one of his own people the following year. Alexander gave him a grand funeral and married his daughter.

Officers and Gentlemen

I am not quite a gentleman but you would hardly notice it but cant be helped anyhow.

Daisy Ashford, *The Young Visiters* (1919), ch. 1

Who first went at it bald-headed?

General John Manners, Marquess of Granby, had the reputation of being a typical aristocrat of his day – fond of sport and gambling – but unlike many of his contemporaries he combined this with genuine military bravery and a wholly untypical concern for the well-being of his soldiers. The first of these traits came to the fore during the Seven Years War – a confusing affair concerning just about every European power of the day and its colonies, and costing the lives of about 1 million men for no readily apparent reason.

John Manners entered the fray as a colonel in the Royal Horse Guards (the Blues) in 1758 and soon made a reputation for himself as hugely brave, if rather poor at administration. Most notably, he led the cavalry charge that stormed Warburg in Germany on 31 July 1760, driving back the French under the command of Lieutenant General Le Chevalier du Muy. According to the regiment, so notable was Manners' performance that day that it led to a new phrase entering the English language.

Manners had been nearly bald from early adulthood and famously refused to wear a wig, even though that was de rigueur at the time, even for people with a full head of hair. Such boldness over baldness was rather admired by those who knew him but it did have one unexpected side-effect. During the Battle of Warburg, Manners led his men in three furious dashes at the French troops during one of which his hat, which was disinclined to remain clamped on his smooth head, flew off. Manners was not a man to swerve from battle, however, and he continued to charge forward, his shiny head gleaming in the sun. Indeed, so impressive did his men find his fearless, and hairless, attack that they coined the phrase, 'going at it bald-headed', in memory of him. The Blues also became the only regiment to allow saluting by all ranks even when not wearing a headdress, in token of this memorable scene.

Old soldiers also remembered Manners in another way. As their commanding officer, he was renowned for his generosity. Indeed,

Walpole said of him: 'Of money he seemed to conceive no use but in giving it away: but that profusion was so indiscriminate, that compassion or solicitation, and consequently imposture, were equally the master of his purse.'

This largesse of spirit saw him tending his own wounded troops in battle, a scene that inspired Edward Penny to paint *The Marquess of Granby Relieving a Sick Soldier*, the engraving of which outsold even the celebrated *Death of General Wolfe*. It also prompted Manners to make financial provision for those of his non-commissioned officers who were forced from his service through injury. Rather than merely appeal to the government for their pensions, Granby set up many of these men as publicans so that they could make their own living. In return these old soldiers named their pubs 'The Marquess of Granby' (often misspelt using the French form 'Marquis'), which explains why even today there are so many pubs bearing that particular name.

Who are the Emperor's Chambermaids?

The 14th Light Dragoons might have been called many things, particularly by the French after their role in the defeat of French forces in the Peninsular War, but their favourite nickname was also their strangest.

It was during the Battle of Vitoria in northern Spain, on 21 June 1813, that the 14th Light Dragoons, along with their comrades in the 18th Light Dragoons, fell in with the baggage train of Napoleon's brother, Joseph Bonaparte. The battle was favouring the British, with the French army in full retreat. Even the imperial baggage had been left behind in the hurried withdrawal, containing what was described as 'the loot of a kingdom'. When the troops came face to face with the extraordinary wealth of the French emperor and his entourage, pursuit of the enemy soon turned to pursuit of riches, and an unseemly scene of unbridled plundering began.

In the circumstances, even the head of the most supposedly

loyal and sober trooper would have been turned, when you consider that the estimated value of the baggage was around £1 million, or £100 million in today's money. The ensuing free-for-all caused consternation among the British High Command, leading Wellington, their commander, to describe his victorious men rather harshly as 'the scum of the earth'. When it came to the 18th Light Dragoons, he was even more piqued, calling them 'a disgrace to the name of soldier, in action as well as elsewhere; and I propose to draft their horses from them and send the men to England if I cannot get the better of them in any other manner.'

But such un-British behaviour as looting and name-calling was not to last. Slowly discipline was restored and the treasures of the emperor were handed over to their rightful new owner – the British government. All except one. Whilst the 18th were getting it in the neck from Wellington, the 14th had managed to slip away with their own prize: a solid silver chamber pot, said to have been a gift from Napoleon himself to his brother Joseph. They had no intention of returning this trophy, which they named 'the Emperor' and took to displaying at dinner, receiving the nickname 'the Emperor's Chambermaids' in the process. And the King's Royal Hussars, successors to the 14th, still have 'the Emperor' to this day, which the commanding officer may invite his comrades to drink from on mess nights.

Who dressed as a nun for the Duke of Wellington?

Colonel Dan MacKinnon, lieutenant colonel in command of the Coldstream Guards, was, as you might expect, the perfect English gentleman soldier, as the tales recounted in his obituary in the *Gentleman's Magazine* for August 1837 suggest.

'Dan' as he was known to his men was reportedly calm under attack. During the Peninsular War, his regiment was advancing under heavy fire. As his column marched forward, he was seen to be shaving in a small shard of mirror to ensure he was properly turned out for battle. Dan was also a heroic man of action, prepared to go where no other soldier would. The *Gentleman's Magazine* tells a 'fearful' story:

> On another occasion, a fir tree had fallen across the sides of a frightful chasm, several hundred feet in depth; it was deemed expedient, if possible, to get on the other side of the abyss; no one would venture to put even a foot on the tree which was extended across, and seemed likely to break in the middle; and even if strong enough to bear a man's weight, could not afford sufficiently secure footing for the purpose. Capt D. MacKinnon advanced, and in a moment ran across it to the other side, which feat was, perhaps, more frightful and appalling to the army than any he had before achieved.

Dan's athleticism came from his youthful habits in London, where he had trained himself by clambering over furniture in clubs and country houses, climbing to the ceiling of rooms and over rooftops 'like a monkey', as Captain Gronow of the Grenadiers put it. He was also a practical joker and on one occasion persuaded a Spanish mayor to entertain him in the belief that he was the Duke of York (although this landed MacKinnon on a charge). In a further adventure he impersonated a nun at a Spanish convent that the Duke of Wellington had wished to visit. Dan, clean shaven and wimpled, was declared by the British party to be one of the most handsome women there before the trick was discovered. It is not known quite what else Dan got up to in the nunnery as Captain Gronow, who recounts the tale, adds: 'I might say more about Dan's adventures in the convent, but have no wish to be scandalous.'

Perhaps not surprisingly, dangerous Dan found his way to the Battle of Waterloo and the very hottest part of the action there, but despite the desperate nature of the fighting he never let his manners slip. Leading a charge against the French, he received a shot to the knee, which, having rendered his leg useless, travelled on into his horse, killing it beneath him. Dan tumbled to the ground in terrible agony only to find his fall broken by a French officer yet more seriously wounded than himself. Dan apologised profusely before telling his wounded opponent that he would, regrettably, have to 'borrow' his sword, as he had misplaced his own in the fall. He added that he hoped the two of them might sup together that night when the battle was over, before excusing himself, pulling himself upright and hobbling back into the action. He then proceeded to defend the Hugoumont farm in the fiercest fighting of the day, before, with the French beaten, he finally succumbed to the delirium of pain and was evacuated to Brussels.

Sadly, the extraordinary, Flashman-like actions of Dan MacKinnon took a toll on him. The wounds he received, together with the effects of yellow fever, which he caught during the Peninsular War, undermined his health. He died in 1837 aged only forty-six.

What were Frederick's three questions?

Stories are legion of Frederick II of Prussia's kindness and rapport with his soldiers, although this is perhaps only to be expected of the son of Frederick William I – known as 'The Soldier King', a man whose brutal treatment of his son culminated in forcing him to watch the execution of a childhood friend.

Frederick might have despised his father's brutality, yet he used the resources he had mustered to turn Prussia into a military force to be reckoned with, in the process being hailed by the title of 'Frederick the Great'. It was said of the king that whenever he met a soldier – and there were an awful lot of soldiers in Prussia – he would ask three questions:

How old are you?
How long have you been in my service?
Are you satisfied with your pay and treatment?

Such an interest in the ordinary soldier was highly unusual for the day but probably went a long way in helping Frederick turn his small and disparate country into a world power. However, knowing that these questions were going to be asked tended to put young soldiers into a panic, particularly those who didn't speak German.

On one occasion it was a young French officer in Frederick's service who found himself before the great man, awaiting the three questions. Fortunately he had prepared for this eventuality and, although he couldn't speak a word of German, he had memorised the answers. Frederick, always a little playful when interviewing his men and perhaps a shade suspicious, chose on this occasion to ask the questions in an unusual order.

When he asked, 'How long have you been in my service?' the young man confidently replied, 'Twenty-one years, sir.' This was impressive in a man so clearly still in his early twenties but Frederick pressed on, asking, 'How old are you?' He received the surprising answer, 'One year, sir.' At this point Frederick gave up the unequal struggle and declared, 'Well, clearly one of us has taken leave of his senses.' The French soldier took this to be the third question, to which, quick as a flash, he replied, 'Both, if you please, sir.' Fortunately Frederick saw the funny side and, having cleared up the misunderstanding, asked his questions again, this time in French, much to the soldier's relief.

How did Nelson prove himself armless?

Following the Battle of Calvi in 1794, Horatio Nelson was never again quite the man he once was, having lost an eye in that engagement. He was further diminished at the Battle of Santa Cruz de Tenerife three years later when he lost his right arm. However, despite the often iniquitous terms of service that the navy offered in those days, compensation was available for 'missing parts'.

When Nelson got the opportunity during leave in 1797 he decided to put in a claim for a year's pay as 'smart money', as this compensation was called, for the missing eye. To his astonishment the clerk concerned refused his request on the grounds that he had not brought a doctor's letter attesting that he had actually lost the sight in his eye. This had not been necessary in proving to the Admiralty that he had lost an arm – even the Admiralty could see that he only had one of those – but the eye was different. For that they required proof.

Somewhat vexed, Nelson went off to find a doctor who duly provided the certificate proving his partial blindness. At the same time he obtained another certificate, 'proving' the loss of his arm just in case the Admiralty had second thoughts about that too.

Armed, as it were, with these documents, Nelson returned to the compensation office and presented them to the clerk who, this time, accepted them. When he came to pay over the money, however, he was surprised to find that Nelson, for all his fame, would receive only the pay due to a captain. Perhaps trying to make amends, the clerk suggested that he thought it should have been more. According to his biographer Robert Southey, Nelson, who was now in a somewhat better mood, replied: 'Oh! this is only for an eye. In a few days I shall come for an arm; and in a little time longer, God knows, most probably for a leg.'

As a postscript, the incident with the eye certificate does help to put one myth to rest – that Nelson, as in so many movie depictions, wore an eye patch. Whilst he did indeed sometimes wear a sunshade to protect his good eye, the fact that the Admiralty required proof of his loss of vision in the other eye suggests that he kept his bad eye uncovered and that the eyeball had not been removed, so from outward appearances the damage was not visible.

How did a handshake prevent a hanging?

Among the officer classes there was for centuries a belief that just because one's country was at war didn't mean one had to put aside the rules of gentlemanly behaviour – other than on the battlefield of course. Indeed, in many instances there was more that united officers with their enemy opposites than with their own men. Just how useful this could be was admirably demonstrated by Captain Robert Rollo Gillespie in 1794.

During that year the British were blockading the Caribbean city of Port au Prince, then the capital of the French colony of Saint-Domingue (later Haiti). With the blockade secure, the British commander decided the decent thing to do would be to send two officers into the city under a flag of truce to demand its surrender. The men chosen for this dangerous job were Captain Gillespie and Captain Rowley. Swashbuckling from the word go, the two captains jumped into the sea and swam ashore with their swords clamped between their teeth. Clearly mistaken for a rather small attack party, they were fired upon and arrested as soon as they got ashore.

They had of course been expecting the French to capitulate but instead they were dragged before the French commissioner, Léger Félicité Sonthonax, as prisoners. Worse still, the republican Sonthonax was in no mood to talk, immediately accusing them of being spies and threatening to have them hanged on the spot. Despite their promising start on board a Royal Navy warship, things had scarcely gone to plan for Gillespie and Rowley, whose future looked bleak at best and short at worst. But just then Gillespie noticed that Sonthonax was wearing the discreet insignia of a Freemason on the buttons of his coat. Immediately his spirits were lifted for, though he and Sonthonax might be mortal enemies on the battlefield, they were, far more importantly, both Masons. Once they made one of the 'secret signs' that Freemasons use to identify each other, Sonthonax's attitude changed in a moment. Casting aside his homicidal intentions towards them, he immediately ordered a splendid banquet for his new chums.

Such a volte-face caught even Gillespie by surprise, who was not used to his handshakes having quite such a profound effect. Initially the Royal Navy captains refused the meal, fearing this was some dastardly French trick, but Sonthonax, a Mason first and foremost, tucked in heartily to prove the food and drink were not poisoned. The party eventually spent a very happy evening together. After much merriment, Gillespie and Rowley were taken to the shore with a guard of honour and rowed back to their ships. However, Sonthonax declined the invitation to surrender.

Why was the Duke of Wellington's ball so cold?

In popular mythology – if you believe films like *Carry On Up the Khyber* – the British army of the nineteenth century behaved as though nothing was ever a problem, whatever difficulties and hardships war might place in their path. Astonishingly, this extreme stoicism did have a basis in fact.

During the Peninsular War, the Duke of Wellington received a dispatch telling him that Lieutenant General the Honourable Galbraith Lowry Cole had been awarded the Order of the Bath and would he kindly perform the investiture himself. The Iberian peninsula at this time was not the most congenial of locations for a formal party, owing to the small matter of the war, but Wellington was not one to shirk an official duty.

The Iron Duke had been made Duke of Ciudad Rodrigo the previous year, following his storming of the town. However, never having really done anything to celebrate the fact, he decided to hold a 'grand fête' there – despite the fact that Ciudad Rodrigo was a bombed-out and looted shell.

Of course it would have been vulgar to point this out, so preparations went ahead as though everything was in perfect order. Arrangements were made to requisition all available china and silver cutlery in the region, and every English and local Spanish dignitary, officer and lady was invited, numbering around sixty-five for dinner, with a total of 190 for the evening ball. As there were no proper cooking facilities in the town, it was arranged for the food to be half cooked at Wellington's headquarters at Frenada, some seventeen miles away, and then brought over by mule for reheating. Champagne, claret and port had to be requisitioned from even further afield.

The British army was perfectly used to eating well on campaign so the food and drink was hardly an issue. Providing a suitable ballroom, however, was trickier. Everyone was roped in to help with the preparations. In his private journal the Judge Advocate General attached to the British forces, F.S. Larpent, recorded his role in the affair with typical British sang-froid:

> I helped . . . by making cards for every place at dinner, with corresponding ones for each person, with his name, table, and number of his plate, so there was no bowing and scraping, or pushing for the first table. We got quarters in the ruins; mine would have been a good one in another week, at a priest's, who was repairing his house, but he had just finished a large opening for a French window in the room, and neither sash nor shutter was made, so that I found it considerably airy.

Nor were Larpent's quarters the only 'airy' building in Ciudad Rodrigo. The ballroom had been chosen as one of the better-preserved rooms in the town, and the stripped and scarred walls had been covered in fabric hangings rescued from another building. This made for a sort of tent affair, distracting the eye from the bullet holes and bare plaster. It was harder to get around the huge opening in the ceiling, particularly as it was March, and the coldest day and night anyone could remember.

Nonetheless, as night fell the band struck up, the champagne was opened, Lieutenant General the Honourable Galbraith Lowry Cole received his Order of the Bath, and the company danced until dawn.

The ladies' dancing was commended although Larpent noted that they were '*not very handsome*' – but then there was a war on. During the English country dances, particular care had also to be taken in one corner of the room where there was a large hole in the floor. Always thoughtful of his guests' comfort, the British commander had placed a discreet mat over this and stationed a soldier next to it to prevent anyone falling through.

By dawn the ladies had retired and the men, bored, were reduced to drinking games. Finally, a more martial atmosphere returned with toasts of 'Death to all Frenchmen' being shouted across the shattered room, along with the odd cry of 'Hip, hip, hurrah!' which the British were busy teaching their Spanish counterparts. In all, the evening had been a thoroughly British affair and had gone splendidly. Everyone had been too polite to mention the gaping hole in the roof or the bitter cold that this let in. Wellington himself had stayed dancing (it was too cold to stop) until half past three before riding back to his headquarters. He had a court martial to attend at noon the next day and needed some sleep. Now that the ball was over, he really had to catch up on the war.

What is the shortest dispatch in military history?

Brevity is allegedly the soul of wit, and being concise and to the point is nowhere more needed than in war. The brief dispatch and the pithy telegram are an art in themselves, requiring the sender to give just enough information for the receiver to act upon but nothing more that might be misconstrued.

For some military men the ability to send such messages has formed a cornerstone of their career. Sir Robert Boyd, governor of Gibraltar in the early 1790s, on finding that the fleet heading back to England might sail before he could get his letters on board, scribbled a three-word order to his agent Browne in London, concerning his immediate needs. The note read: 'Browne – Beef – Boyd'. When the next British fleet called in, carrying the required meat, it came with an equally laconic reply from his agent attached to it. This read: 'Boyd – Beef – Browne'.

Perhaps the most famous, informative and terse military telegram is, however, attributed to General Charles Napier. A career soldier, Napier had been sent to the Bombay presidency, a province of British India, by the Directors of the British East India Company in 1841 and in the following year had been put in command of the British army in Sindh, with orders to quell anti-British sentiment among the local rulers of the province. Whilst there was no explicit order given for him to invade Sindh – indeed, Gladstone's cabinet and some of the directors of the East India Company actively opposed such a dangerous extension of their interests – Napier decided to act. He viewed the eighteen or so amirs who ruled the region as feudal relics and determined to remove them by insisting they sign new and onerous treaties with the British. Napier knew that this action was rather unsavoury and admitted, 'We have no right to seize Sind, yet we shall do so, and a very advantageous, useful and humane piece of rascality it will be.'

In return for what he hoped would be substantial prize money, he was quite prepared to put aside any moral objections and do the deed. Having driven the amirs to declare war, he met the enemy at the Battle of Miani with a force of just 2,200 mainly local men and defeated a force of 20,000 soldiers of the Talpur amirs of Sindh. Shortly afterwards, the capital Hyderabad fell and, with it, Sindh itself. It was a spectacular victory. Napier is said to have sent a one-word telegram back to the Court of Directors of the East India Company, reading, 'Peccavi' – the Latin for 'I have sinned', a pun on 'I have Sindh' and a recognition of the morally dubious nature of the victory.

Whether the telegram was actually sent or derived from the satirical *Punch* cartoon of 1842, it seems to have started a spate of Latin puns among the classically educated military leaders of Victorian Britain. In 1855, Lord Dalhousie is credited with the dispatch, 'Vovi' – 'I vowed' – to announce he had taken the state of Oudh. Two years later the more elaborate phrase, 'Nunc fortunatus sum' – 'I am in luck now' – is attributed to Lord Clyde after his capture of Lucknow.

How did the Peasants' Revolt end?

The Peasants' Revolt against the government of Richard II is generally viewed in history as one of the great popular movements against tyranny but the ignominious end of its leader, Wat Tyler, is often left out of the tale.

It was nearly three o'clock on the afternoon of Saturday, 15 June 1381, before King Richard bade his mother farewell and set off for Smithfield with an entourage of about 200 knights, squires and retainers to parley with the leaders of the revolt.

After praying in Westminster Abbey, the king remounted his horse and rode back down the Strand, over Holborn Hill and through the Aldersgate – over which Chaucer was at that time living – and out to Smithfield. Smithfield was a large open space, used occasionally for jousting tournaments but more commonly as a slaughter site, whose associated foul smell always hung faintly in the air. Opposite stood the Hospital and Priory of St Bartholomew which gave its name to the yearly fair held there. When Richard approached at six o'clock, vespers were being sung in the wrecked remains of the Priory. On the field were gathered thousands of the rebels amid a sea of banners and pennants, formed up in battle fashion to the west. Richard and his entourage drew up outside the hospital, facing them.

The king now sent across an envoy, probably the mayor, William Walworth. He announced to the rebels that their sovereign wanted words with their leader. Wat Tyler came forward and mounted his hackney (a small, stocky pony). As he advanced he seemed jovial, perhaps trying to put the young king at his ease. Having dismounted, he half bent his knee in fealty before grabbing the king's hand and vigorously shaking it, saying: 'Brother, be of good cheer. Within a fortnight ye shall have more thanks from the commons than ever before. We twain shall be right good fellows.'

Such forwardness shocked the king's train but Richard remained calm, asking Tyler simply why his men had not disbanded and returned to their homes. Tyler responded, according to one chronicle, with a 'great oath', saying his men would not leave until all their demands had been met. He then listed these to the king. Their exact nature remains unknown as different chronicles offer conflicting accounts but it seems likely that one of them was that all men should be free and equal, none having position over another, save for the king himself. Furthermore all land was to be distributed evenly, although each man should pay 4d per acre to its former owner. There were also grievances against the Church. Tyler probably stipulated that all the bishoprics be disbanded save for one archbishopric and that all church estates be distributed amongst the poor, saving only enough to provide for one priest for each village. He also asked for the repeal of the recent labour legislation, enacted in the wake of the Black Death and designed to prevent peasants from exploiting the labour shortage to improve their conditions.

Had these measures been carried out, they would have radically changed the whole nature of the Church and State. Tyler must have been aware that the king could not and would not accede to them all at that moment. Many were not in the gift of the king anyway but would have required the agreement of parliament. In fact Richard probably had no intention of granting Tyler any of his requests and he gave an evasive reply that he would do all that was right saving the dignity of his crown.

How Tyler reacted is not recorded but the king's reply cannot have been the answer he was looking for. Perhaps he already knew that his cause was hopeless and was rehearsing his ideas for the sake of posterity rather than in the hope of swaying the king. It was a hot evening and his throat was dry after his speech so he called for a mug of water. When this was brought he swilled the water around his mouth and spat it out, much to the disgust of the royal party. He then called for a flagon of beer, which he downed at a draught before remounting his pony. Whether this was a calculated insult or the natural behaviour of a simple man remains a mystery. Certainly his manner seemed coarse in the eyes of the king's faction but that hardly warranted his fate. It is unlikely that he would have deliberately insulted the king if he still held out any hope of gaining concessions from him. Either way, events now overtook him.

As he remounted his pony, a retainer came forward. Seeing Tyler, he exclaimed: 'I know this man, he is the greatest rogue in Kent, a highwayman and a robber.'

The insult seems to have been calculated to have provoked Tyler but, rather than plunge further into the group of Richard's men to find his accuser, he shook his head in denial and asked the man to step forward. The retainer was reluctant but was eventually pushed to the front. Tyler turned to his only escort and told him to cut the man down. The retainer retorted that he had told the truth and that no man deserved to die for that. There is some confusion as to what happened in the next few seconds but Tyler, who had been toying with a dagger throughout the meeting, may have made for the man. Certainly Walworth took the opportunity to put himself between the two and arrested Tyler for drawing a weapon in the presence of the king.

Tyler must have known that there was now little hope of escape. Maddened, he lunged forward with his dagger, striking Walworth in the body. However, like the rest of the royal party, Walworth was wearing a coat of mail under his tunic and the blow did not penetrate. He responded by drawing his own dagger and stabbing Tyler in the neck and shoulder, opening a wide wound. As Tyler slumped forward on his horse, John Standwick, a squire, stepped up and ran him through twice with a sword. Summoning up his last energy, Tyler spurred his horse, which set off back towards the rebels. Halfway across the field he fell dying to the ground. His last word was 'treason'.

There followed an uneasy few seconds. Some of the rebels, seeing their captain murdered, strung their bows and untrussed their sheaves of arrows, but with extraordinary presence of mind the king rode straight out to them and is reported to have said: 'Sirs, will you shoot your king? I will be your chief and captain, you shall have from me that which you seek.' Wanting to distract the crowd from the body of the dead (or dying) Tyler, he then asked them to follow him to the open fields of Clerkenwell. Bewildered, and with no one offering himself as their new leader, the rebels followed the king.

At Clerkenwell, the king stalled for time while Walworth and the king's knights returned to London as fast as they could. Here they gathered a force of around 5,000 men in so short a time as to make it likely that they had been prepared beforehand. This host rode out to join the king. At Smithfield, Walworth was perplexed to find that Tyler's body was not lying where it fell on the field. After a brief search, he was found in the Hospital of St Bartholomew where his friends had taken him to tend his wounds. Walworth had no such compassion and ordered Tyler to be dragged out of the hospital and back onto the field. Here he was laid, perhaps already dead, over a log and beheaded. With Tyler's head on a pike, Walworth and his men made for Richard at Clerkenwell. As the rebels, already dazed and confused, saw the soldiers draw near, holding above them their leader's bleeding head, they must have known that the revolt, at least in London, was over. In the words of the near-contemporary *Anonimales Chronicle*: 'And when the Commons saw their chieftain, Wat Tyghler, was dead in such a manner, they fell to the ground there among the corn, like beaten men.'

Richard did grant the rebels an amnesty, against the advice of Walworth and others, who urged that all the insurgents at Smithfield be slaughtered as an example to others. That night most of them slipped off back to their homes, with their charters revoked and their cause lost.

for Valour

Mutual cowardice keeps us in peace. Were one half of mankind brave and one half cowards, the brave would be always beating the cowards. Were all brave, they would lead a very uneasy life; all would be continually fighting: but being all cowards, we go on very well.

Samuel Johnson, quoted by James Boswell, *The Life of Samuel Johnson* (1791), 28 April 1778

How did Lord Uxbridge's leg become famous?

Henry Paget, 2nd Earl of Uxbridge, has gone down in history as one of the most stiff-upper-lipped of all stiff-upper-lipped Englishmen. Being promoted by Wellington on the eve of the Battle of Waterloo to command the whole of the Allied cavalry and horse artillery, he proved intent on leading from the front. This was undoubtedly inspiring but it was also dangerous.

The following day, 18 June 1815, Uxbridge led a spectacular cavalry charge against the French I *corps d'armée*, followed by a series of light-cavalry charges, during which eight horses were shot from under him. Undeterred, he continued to wade into the battle until one of the last French artillery shots of the day struck him on the right leg. The cannon in question was loaded with grapeshot and the leg in question was completely shattered. A lesser man might have been expected to let out a small squeal at this point but not the Earl of Uxbridge. According to anecdote, Wellington was near by at the time and Uxbridge, looking down at the bloody remains of his leg, commented, 'By God, sir, I've lost my leg!' to which Wellington replied, 'By God, sir, so you have!'

This is, of course, mere anecdote but what happened next suggests that such a response would be quite within Uxbridge's repertoire. The injured earl withdrew to the village of Waterloo where a medical orderly examined him in the house of Monsieur Hyacinthe Joseph-Marie Paris, who, despite the fact that one of the largest battles in history was blazing on his doorstep, had decided that this was no reason for him to leave his home. Uxbridge was now told the leg would have to be amputated, without of course the aid of antiseptics or anaesthetics. This would be enough to make many a grown man weak but, according to his aide-de-camp, who was there, he simply replied, 'I have had a pretty long run. I have been a beau these forty-seven years, and it would not be fair to cut the young men out any longer.'

And so the leg was removed as Uxbridge sat in his chair, his only further comment on the operation being a blood-curdling,

'The knives seem rather blunt.' After the procedure, the earl began to have second thoughts, however, and when his friend Sir Vivian Hussey came in to see him, he was reported as saying: 'Ah, Vivian, I want you to do me a favour. Some of my friends here seem to think I might have kept that leg on. Just go and cast your eye upon it, and tell me what you think.'

Quite what poor Sir Vivian was meant to say in response is uncertain but, with the sort of pluck that seemed to characterise the day, he later wrote: 'I went, accordingly and, taking up the lacerated limb, carefully examined it, and so far as I could tell, it was completely spoiled for work. A rusty grape-shot had gone through and shattered the bones all to pieces. I therefore returned to the Marquis and told him he could set his mind quite at rest, as his leg, in my opinion, was better off than on.' On hearing this, Uxbridge was greatly relieved.

This extraordinary display of phlegm not surprisingly made Uxbridge famous. The saw that removed the offending limb was lovingly preserved and is now in the British Army Museum. Uxbridge himself was offered an annual pension of £1,200 as compensation. Naturally he refused.

Monsieur Paris, with an eye to business, asked whether he could keep the leg, which he did, burying it in his garden with its own tombstone. Here it became something of a shrine. M. Paris charged visiting dignitaries to see it until, in 1878, it was discovered that the bones themselves were now on show in the house, sparking a diplomatic incident. The British demanded that the leg be repatriated but the Paris family refused, even offering to sell it back to the Uxbridges who refused as they considered it to be one of their legs anyway. The French government eventually ordered the leg reburied but instead it was hidden, finally coming to light in 1934 when the widow of the last M. Paris found it in a box in her husband's study. Thoroughly sick of the trouble the wandering limb had caused, she threw the remains into the fire.

How did Turkish sang-froid impress the British?

The Battle of Navarino on 20 October 1827 is known in history as the last major naval action fought entirely with sailing ships. In this bloody and bruising action, a combined British, French and Russian fleet destroyed the Ottoman Turkish and Egyptian fleets in Navarino Bay, in the Greek Peloponnese. It led to some remarkable tales of Turkish sang-froid making their way back to Britain.

Two of these occur in *Life on Board a Man of War*, written by 'A British sailor' and published in 1829. The first tells of one George Finney who was detailed to row a British boat that was picking up survivors from sunken ships. Having hauled one dishevelled Turk aboard, George expected to receive profuse thanks from one who might otherwise have drowned. To his amazement, his captive simply pulled a waterproof bundle from his clothes and unwrapped a pipe, which he began to smoke, blowing clouds of Turkish tobacco fumes over his rescuer. Whilst nobody would begrudge a man a quiet smoke after so close a brush with death, the Turk's apparent indifference to his predicament earned the ire of George Finney who promptly pushed him back in.

Cooler still was the grandly dressed Turk who was fished out of the water by the boat of the French frigate *Alcyone*. He was brought aboard the French ship where it became immediately evident that one of his arms had been completely smashed and would need to be amputated. Undeterred by the unfortunate situation he now found himself in, the injured sailor was reported to have marched down the frigate deck as though he had made a prize of the ship himself, descended the cockpit ladder one-handed with as much grace and skill as most sailors managed with two hands, and found the ship's surgeon. He then gestured that he wanted the shattered arm removed and the surgeon obliged, without anaesthetic of course. After the stump was cleaned and bound, the Turkish sailor then returned to the deck and promptly jumped overboard, swimming back to his own ship, which was, even as these events had been unfolding, firing on the *Alcyone*. The last anyone saw of this remarkable man was as he hauled himself back aboard his ship. Moments later it took a hit to its magazine and the whole vessel exploded, rendering the French surgeon's work rather unnecessary.

Which blind king gave the Prince of Wales his motto?

No one could accuse John I of Bohemia of being a coward. Rash, possibly, but not a coward. John, son of the Holy Roman Emperor Henry VII, was the count of Luxembourg, the king of Bohemia and the titular king of Poland, making him rather a big cheese in early fourteenth-century European politics. He was a political animal and a fighter but his career in the latter role had come to something of an abrupt end after a bout of ophthalmia, contracted during a season crusading with the Teutonic Knights in Lithuania, left him almost completely blind.

Most kings at this stage would have retired from the front line, but not John. That was a mistake, as the last front line he found himself on was facing the British troops of Edward III and his son, the Black Prince, at the Battle of Crécy on 26 August 1346. John, as an ally of the French, was not having a good day. The French knights of Philip VI had proved overconfident and despite repeated charges had failed to break the English line, coming, all the time, under withering fire from the English long-bowmen.

As the battle progressed, John watched, or rather listened, from the sidelines, becoming increasingly aware of the fact that, although the French had huge superiority in numbers, they were decisively losing. It is not to be wondered at that his thoughts turned to his son who had joined him on the battlefield that day. As the chronicler Jean Froissart tells it: 'The valiant king of Bohemia called John of Luxembourg, son to the noble emperor Henry of Luxembourg, for all that he was nigh blind, when he understood the order of the battle, he said to them about him:

"Where is the lord Charles my son?" His men said: "Sir, we cannot tell; we think he be fighting."'

Nobody knows quite where Charles actually was at this point but we know he did survive the battle. There is a hint in Froissart that he might have run away: 'The lord Charles of Bohemia his son . . . came in good order to the battle; but when he saw that the matter went awry on their party, he departed, I cannot tell you which way.'

His father was made of sterner stuff, however. Hearing that his son was probably in the thick of the action, John decided it was time to join the fray. This of course would be tricky as, being blind, he would need guidance if he was to attack knights on horseback with his sword. Undaunted, he told his men: 'Sirs, ye are my men, my companions and friends in this journey: I require you bring me so far forward, that I may strike one stroke with my sword.'

How could his faithful retainers argue with such a courageous request? 'They said they would do his commandment, and to the intent that they should not lose him in the press, they tied all their reins of their bridles each to other and set the king before to accomplish his desire, and so they went on their enemies.'

And so, all tied together, blind John and his two faithful knights headed into combat, the king swinging his sword about him. But the battle was already hopelessly lost. Some 30,000 troops of Philip and his allies were dead by the end of the day, compared to around 200 English casualties. The next morning the inevitable discovery was made: 'And they adventured themselves so forward, that they were there all slain, and the next day they were found in the place about the king, and all their horses tied each to other.'

It is said, although there is no conclusive proof, that the Black Prince took the feathered crest from the helmet of the fallen John of Bohemia, along with his motto 'Ich Dien', and made them the crest and motto of the princes of Wales, which they retain to this day.

Who was Black Agnes?

On 13 January 1338, the army of Edward III, keen to avenge their disastrous defeat at the hands of the Scots twenty-four years earlier at Bannockburn, drew up outside the heavy gates of Dunbar castle in East Lothian, Scotland. For the Earl of Salisbury, who commanded the English force, the castle presented a relatively easy target. Despite its strength, its owner, Patrick Dunbar, 9th Earl of Dunbar and March, was away to the north and the defences were under the command of his twenty-six-year-old wife who was, after all, a mere woman.

What Salisbury didn't know was that this mere woman – Lady Agnes Randolph, Countess of Moray, who, thanks to her dark hair and complexion, was known as Black Agnes – had sworn to defend the castle to the death. When the order to surrender came from the English, she replied, according to the old Scottish rhyme:

> Of Scotland's King I haud my house,
> He pays me meat and fee,
> And I will keep my gude auld house,
> While my house will keep me.

Of course Agnes probably didn't actually go to the lengths of putting her riposte into rhyme but the message was certainly the same. Not that this daunted Salisbury who was one of the most experienced military commanders of the day. He simply drew up his siege engines and began pounding the walls of Dunbar with his mangonels – catapults capable of launching huge boulders. The effect it produced was something of a surprise, however. In the lull between each volley of fire, the attackers noticed people on the battlements, who on closer inspection were discovered to be not soldiers but maids in their best Sunday dresses. Black Agnes, to show her scorn for the bombardment, was sending her maids onto the walls to dust away the battle damage between attacks.

Such nonchalance suggested to Salisbury that he was perhaps not dealing with your average chatelaine and so he pulled another trick from his hat. In his baggage train he had a huge battering ram protected from above by a wooden roof. This monster, known as the 'sow', was now wheeled up. As Salisbury saw it, the gates would be down in a matter of moments and the siege at an end, regardless of Agnes's furious dusting.

Once again the Englishman had underestimated his foe. As the sow was brought forward, Agnes ordered that the rocks and lead that had been collected from the English artillery assault be gathered together over the entrance. These were then 'returned' to their owners by being rolled over the battlements, smashing the sow to smithereens beneath them.

Increasingly exasperated, Salisbury tried a more personal tack. Having captured Agnes's brother, John Randolph, 3rd Earl of Moray, he had him paraded before the castle with a rope around his neck. A message was then conveyed into the castle, warning that he would be hanged unless the chatelaine of Dunbar opened the gates immediately. But if Salisbury hoped to appeal to Agnes's familial sensibilities, he was wrong again. She sent back the message that they should go ahead and kill her brother as that would leave her as the inheritor of the earldom of Moray. Fortunately for John Randolph, the English believed that Black Agnes might indeed be that calculating and didn't execute the earl after all. Agnes won another game of brinkmanship.

Eventually, on 10 June, after nearly five months of siege, Black Agnes awoke to find that the English were preparing to strike camp and go home. What should have been a quick and decisive victory had turned into a fiasco. A woman had beaten the best commander in England. Despite every stratagem, she had proved a match for Salisbury. The later ballad writers put these weary words into the mouth of the defeated man: 'Cam I early, cam I late, there was Agnes at the gate.'

How can you become a war hero without lifting a gun?

The most highly decorated NCO of the First World War was Lance Corporal William Harold Coltman, who came out of the conflict with a Victoria Cross, two Distinguished Conduct medals, two military medals and a fistful of mentions in dispatches. What is more remarkable is that he was a conscientious objector.

Coltman, who had worked as a gardener before the war, joined up in 1915, following in the footsteps of his four brothers. So, aged twenty-four, he was sent to France as part of the 1/6th Territorial battalion of the North Staffordshire (Prince of Wales's) regiment.

Once in the trenches, Coltman found himself in something of a quandary as he was a member of the Brethren Sect and his very strong religious beliefs made him unwilling to kill. Life for a conscientious objector in the First World War was not pleasant as, with so many young men going to their deaths, every effort was made to ensure that those who refused to fight didn't have an easy ride, if, indeed, they were not simply branded as cowards and sent to the front anyway. Coltman, however, was no coward; in fact he had volunteered, despite his beliefs. Nevertheless, he represented a problem for his commanding officer until he agreed to a non-combatant role as a regimental stretcher-bearer to 'A' company.

For some this might be seen as licence to keep one's head down and see out the war, but for Coltman it was a chance to prove that saving life can be more heroic than taking it. He soon became a familiar face on the front line and in no man's land, tending the wounded and dying under constant fire, his only protection being the Red Cross armband he always wore. His final great accolade came on 4 October 1918, just a month before the end of the war, during an operation to the north of Saint Quentin.

The citation for his Victoria Cross reads:

> For most conspicuous bravery, initiative and devotion to duty. During the operations at Mannequin Hill, north-east of

> Sequehart, on the 3rd and 4th of Oct. 1918, L.-Corp. Coltman, a stretcher bearer, hearing that wounded had been left behind during the retirement, went forward alone in the face of fierce enfilade fire, found the casualties, dressed their wounds and on three successive occasions, carried some of them on his back to safety, thus saving their lives. This very gallant NCO then tended the wounded unceasingly for 48 hours.

Coltman survived both world wars, living to the age of eighty-two, having proved that the only thing more heroic than bearing arms into battle is not bearing them.

How did Haile Selassie motivate his troops?

There comes a moment in the history of many countries when the danger posed by an enemy is so great that it is not enough simply to send your standing army into battle – assuming you have one in the first place. Instead the people as a whole must be called upon and, through a combination of appeals to their patriotism and implicit threats should they refuse, be encouraged to sign up and fight for their homes.

Getting your population to fight, and organising them when you do, is no mean feat, however. Kitchener achieved great fame with his 'Your Country Needs You' posters, although this was never actually used as an official recruiting poster in the First World War, becoming famous only after the war when foreign imitators, notably the USA, took up the design. The stern old warhorse pointing a summoning finger went on to become one of the most powerful recruiting images in history, leading society hostess Margot Asquith to quip that if Kitchener were not a great man, 'He was at least a great poster.'

For Haile Selassie, as he prepared to fight off the Italian invasion of Ethiopia in 1935, there was little time to appeal to patriotism. The Italian army invaded in October of that year without declaring war, making extensive use of (illegal) mustard gas to quell any opposition. The European powers, keen not to drive Italy into the hands of the Germans, looked on ambivalently while slow diplomatic manoeuvres took place at the League of Nations. Selassie had little choice but to get his people to fight and fight now, and so he issued one of the most abrupt and wide-ranging mobilisation orders of all time:

1. Everyone will now be mobilised.
2. All boys old enough to carry a spear will be sent to Addis Ababa.
3. Married men will take their wives to carry food and cook.
4. Single men will take any woman without a husband.
5. Women with small babies need not go.
6. The blind and those who cannot walk or carry a spear are excused.
7. Anyone found at home after receipt of this order will be hanged.

The threat of immediate execution did the trick and around 500,000 men answered the call. Equipped largely with agricultural implements and a few nineteenth-century rifles, these untrained conscripts were vastly outclassed. On 7 May 1936, Italy annexed Ethiopia and two days later the Italian king, Victor Emmanuel II, was declared emperor of the new state of Italian East Africa.

How did Totila the Ostrogoth play for time?

One of the hardest decisions a general has to make is deciding when to fight. Should he wait until he has all the forces he needs or surprise the enemy with a pre-emptive strike whilst risking fighting under strength? Never is this decision more pressing than when facing a 20,000-strong Roman army.

This was the situation of Totila, king of the Ostrogoths, on the morning of the Battle of Taginae in late June 552. The army that Totila was facing had been sent to wrest Italy from his control by the Eastern emperor Justinian I and outnumbered his own force by perhaps 5,000 men. Initial manoeuvrings had not favoured the Ostrogoths and an attempt to outflank their enemy had failed, whilst the Roman forces had managed to take up a strong central position flanked by thousands of Byzantine archers. The two armies now stood face to face, awaiting the order to attack.

It was at this moment that Totila received news that reinforcements under his commander Teia were near by. The prospect of getting another 2,000 men was tempting but with individual challenges between soldiers on each side already taking place, how could he delay the battle long enough for them to arrive?

The answer he came up with was not perhaps what one would expect from an Ostrogoth. He put on a cabaret show. Riding out into no man's land between the armies in his best gold-plated armour, and with dancing purple plumes in his helmet, he began giving a demonstration of horsemanship, twisting and turning his mount in a series of prancing spins and jumps. He then moved on to the main part of his act – a demonstration of spear handling, spinning the weapon in his hands, throwing it high into the air and catching it, sometimes left-handed, sometimes right-handed, in what can only be described as a baton-twirling display. After that it was back to the horse tricks, jumping on and off his mount from a standing start.

Exactly what his enemy, or indeed his friends, thought about this show isn't recorded by the Roman historian Procopius who memorialised the scene, but he does tell us that it went on for most of the morning. By now the armies were perhaps getting a bit fed up with his exhibitionism for suddenly he changed tack. Having either run out of energy or material, he abruptly asked to negotiate, but the Roman commander Nares, then seventy-four, refused, pointing out that the presence of his large army suggested that he was quite keen to do battle.

At this juncture news finally came to Totila that Teia had arrived with his men, at which point he and his army marched off the battlefield and went for lunch.

The extraordinary show of the morning and the sudden departure for din-dins do of course beg the question: why didn't the Roman army just attack, either during the show or when the enemy retired for refreshments? The answer was made very clear that afternoon. Totila tried a surprise attack immediately after the meal was over but found the Romans had kept in their positions, eating where they stood. They had remained in place because they knew they had the advantage of the terrain and Totila would eventually have to attack them there. In fact, he had frittered away his morning entertaining them as they had no intention of leaving their position and were just waiting for him to make a move. When he finally did, the Roman flanking archers curled round his attacking force, directing withering fire onto them. The Ostrogothic army was annihilated and Totila was killed.

Who left his skin in his will?

For millennia the drum has been one of the favoured instruments to carry into battle but Jan Zizka had a novel idea for how it might help his troops even after his death.

The burning at the stake in 1415 of the religious reformer Jan Hus sparked a major uprising in Bohemia against the monarchy and the Church, which brought to the fore the one-eyed Hussite general, Jan Zizka. At the outbreak of the Hussite Wars in 1419, Zizka had to work out how to turn an army that consisted almost entirely of peasants into a force able to take on the Holy Roman Empire and the papacy, which considered them heretics. His success in doing this made him a legend. Quite literally, he forged his peasants' ploughshares into swords and their flails into maces. He was also perhaps the first military leader to form his wagons into a circle to protect his troops from ambush – a lesson later well learnt in the 'Wild West'. Some of these wagons were even armoured and used as platforms for small artillery pieces – a primitive forerunner of the tank.

Zizka's campaigning culminated in the spectacular defeat of

the Holy Roman Emperor Sigismund at the Battle of Nebovidy on 6 January 1422, but the opportunity to bring a lasting peace was wasted when the various religious factions descended into civil war, giving their enemies a chance to prepare and launch a third 'crusade' against them. Undaunted, and even after losing his other eye, Zizka continued to fight, against both Sigismund and the various factions at home. Having boldly, but unsuccessfully, invaded Hungary, he marched on his own capital of Prague, eventually bringing about a peace agreement at home. Then, just as he was preparing to invade Hungary's ally, Moravia, Zizka was taken ill with plague and died.

As he had not only held together his country's defence against the emperor and the pope, but also steered Bohemia out of civil war, his influence at the time of his death was almost unimaginable. His own people began to refer to themselves as 'the orphans', while Bohemians of all religious persuasions wondered what or who could now protect them from the Hungarians and, indeed, each other. But, according to the anti-Hussite Aeneas Sylvius, also known as Pope Pius II – who happens to be the only reigning pope ever to write an autobiography – Zizka had one final gift for them:

> The one whom no mortal hand could destroy was extinguished by the finger of God. As he lay ill, he was asked where he wished to be buried after his death. He ordered that his body be flayed, the flesh discarded for the birds and animals and a drum be fashioned from his skin. With this drum in the lead they should go to war. The enemies would turn to flight as soon as they heard its sound.

Which Russian ace looked a gift horse in the mouth?

In the Second World War many women took to the air, delivering aircraft to the front line and flying support missions, although only the Russian airforce actually formed a squadron of female fighter pilots, among whom few could compare with the extraordinary ace Lydia Vladimirovna Litvyak.

Litvyak had learned to fly before the war and held a flight instructor's licence at the outbreak of hostilities with Germany in 1941. She immediately applied for active service but was taken on only after doctoring her flight log to add 100 hours' more flying time than she actually had. At the age of twenty-one she was posted to the unique, all-female, 586th Fighter regiment and first flew against the enemy in 1942, showing such skill in handling a plane, and such an innate grasp of aerial combat, that she was, in September of that year, transferred to a male unit, the 296th, fighting in the skies over Stalingrad. It was here that she made her first 'kill' and here too that the petite flyer gained the nickname 'the rose of Stalingrad'.

By early 1943 she was becoming something of a celebrity at home. She had recently married the Russian fighter ace Aleksey Solomatin and her own increasing kill tally made them a unique fighter-ace couple. In February her contribution was recognised by the state with the award of a Red Star order but, outside the Soviet Union, her achievements remained virtually unknown, particularly in Germany. This led to perhaps the most famous exchange in her short life.

It was sometimes the case with fighter pilots, that aircrew whom they had shot down and who were subsequently captured might be introduced to their nemesis. Thus it was that one day Litvyak found herself face to face with a German pilot. She explained that she had brought down his plane and hoped that he had not been badly injured in the process. The response was not, however, what she might have hoped. The pilot absolutely refused to believe that he had been bested by a woman, something that he felt only added to his humiliation. It was only after Litvyak took him through every twist and turn of their dogfight that he finally conceded that it must have been her. Abashed, and perhaps wanting to do the best thing in a difficult situation, the German summoned up his best 'Blue Max' spirit and, saluting Litvyak, took off his gold watch and offered it to her. It was not a good decision. Litvyak fixed him with a stare and announced, 'I do not accept gifts from my enemies,' before walking out of the interview.

As with so many fighter pilots, tragedy was only just around the corner for Litvyak. In May 1943 her husband was killed crash-landing his badly shot up plane. Litvyak had also by this time been wounded herself and was soon after wounded again. By the summer she was mentally and physically exhausted but she continued to fly. On 1 August she was finally shot down in combat but, without firm evidence as to her fate, she was simply posted as 'missing'. In fact she was dead, her aircraft being located only in 1979. After further investigations proved she had died in the crash, she was made a 'Hero of the Soviet Union' in 1990, credited with eleven kills.

Between the Devil and the Deep Blue Sea

Naval tradition? Monstrous. Nothing but rum, sodomy, prayers, and the lash.

Winston Churchill, quoted in *Diary of Harold Nicolson* (2004), 17 August 1950

Why did Captain Müller keep quiet?

Just before dawn on 5 October 1914, the German light cruiser *Emden* and its collier dropped anchor in the lagoon of the tiny Indian Ocean atoll of Diego Garcia. To say this was an 'out of the way' place would be an understatement. Diego Garcia, a British dependency, lies 1,600 kilometres south of India and, at the time, had neither telegraph nor any other means of communication with the outside world, save for the regular schooner service that stopped off once every three months. The arrival of two large vessels in the lagoon was therefore a cause for celebration.

No one was more pleased than the plantation manager, Mr Spender, who hoped the fine cruiser now at anchor in the sound might be a British ship, bringing news of the mother country and supplies. His uncertainty stemmed from the fact that the ship was not flying any colours. When he clambered aboard and was greeted by the captain, it soon became clear that the *Emden* was German. However, any ship was an honoured guest at the island and Captain Karl von Müller proved a more than civilised host. Brandy was drunk and cigars smoked late into the night. Müller told Spender the news from the wider world – for example, that Pope Pius X had died – and Mr Spender explained a little of life in this remote spot.

By the end of the evening the two men had agreed how the ship and island might help each other a little before parting. The *Emden* had been cruising the Indian Ocean since 10 September and was keen to resupply with fresh fruit, vegetables and meat, which Diego Garcia could provide. The vessel also needed to make some running repairs. Its hull had become fouled with barnacles and needed careening (scraping) but this was a major job (see page 78 for just how badly wrong this can go). Captain Müller suggested that perhaps they could careen afloat in the still waters of the lagoon by flooding the port and starboard compartments in turn to heel the ship on one side, then the other. If the people of Diego would help scrape the hull, they would all be rewarded.

Diego Garcia was a poor island and the offer of well-paid work was more than welcome.

So for the next few days the crew of the *Emden* and the people of Diego Garcia worked handsomely together. Provisions were brought, the hull was careened, the superstructure was repainted a fetching grey and all the minor running repairs were carried out. Captain Müller even found time to send some of his engineers to recover the island's own defunct launch, which they repaired as a present for the islanders.

Finally, at eleven o'clock on 10 October, a typical sunny Diego Garcia morning, the work was done. Having exchanged gifts, the *Emden* and its collier slipped their lines and steamed north-west, out into the Indian ocean. On board Karl von Müller was delighted. The British subjects of the island could not have been more accommodating. True, he had omitted to tell them about the outbreak of the First World War but that would only have complicated matters. If they had tried to resist he would have been forced to shell the defenceless island and take what he needed anyway. Now he could return to his mission, attacking British shipping. His luck, however, was finally running out and, with sixty Allied warships now searching for him, the *Emden* would be sunk in less than a month.

On Diego Garcia everyone had also been charmed by their civilised German guests. It was only when the British warship, HMS *Hampshire*, and the auxiliary cruiser, *Empress of Russia*, called at the islands two days later, and enquired whether the locals had seen the German warship that was terrorising British supply lines, that the inhabitants had bashfully to admit that they had. Sadly, as no one had seen fit to inform them of the outbreak of war, they had let her go.

How did the captain of U-1206 sink his boat?

The call of nature is one of the facts of life that must be dealt with by the designer of every war vehicle that requires manning.

On a ship it's easy as, in the last resort, there's always the sea. In a small plane you might have to hold on but there's always the comforting thought that no flight can last more than a few hours. A submarine is more problematic. Submarine crews might be submerged for many hours or days at a time and the crew will simply have to go to the lavatory but they obviously can't just go over the side.

The solution hit upon by U-boat crews in the Second World War was the high-pressure submarine toilet, a fiendishly complicated device that directed waste from the toilet bowl through a series of chambers to an airlock where, with a puff of compressed air, it was expelled from the boat into the surrounding sea.

Using the high-pressure toilet was in fact so complex that it required special training. The operative had to remember the exact order in which to open and close various valves to ensure the waste went out and the sea didn't come in. And so we come to 14 April 1945 aboard the U-1206 as it cruised at a depth of 200 feet some ten miles off Peterhead in the North Sea.

The U-1206 had had an uneventful career since her launch in December 1943. She had not sunk or damaged a single ship, nor had she lost a single member of her crew, but all this was about to change as Captain Karl-Adolph Schlitt had decided to answer a call of nature. What exactly happened when he finished and flushed is a matter for debate; indeed, there are two schools of thought. The first, as told to a German researcher by Captain Schlitt himself, was that the toilet malfunctioned. The second, more widely reported, had it that the bashful captain refused to call the crew member who had been trained in high-pressure toilet use and instead had a go at operating it himself. In his confusion he got the order of valves wrong. The result was the same, whether through misadventure or malfunction, and Schlitt was instantly showered with high-pressure sewage and sea water, which began flooding into the toilet compartment.

Pandemonium ensued. By the time the valves had been shut, sea water was draining through the lavatory compartment into the battery room below. When the water came into contact with the battery acid, it began forming highly toxic chlorine gas. Schlitt was forced to give the order to surface to vent the sub. At this point you will remember that the U-1206 was only ten miles off Peterhead and, as it surfaced, it was almost immediately spotted by a British aircraft and bombed. Schlitt, unable to escape, was forced to burn his orders and scuttle his submarine, making his the only submarine ever to be sunk by its own toilet.

How much rum does it take to sink a battleship?

To say that the *Royal George* was a magnificent ship would, in its day, have been an understatement. Originally laid down as the *Royal Anne* but renamed in honour of the reigning King George II at her launch in 1756, she cost £65,000, and was the first warship in excess of 2,000 tons, a first-rate, 100-gun ship of the line, and a veteran of the battles of Cape St Vincent and Quiberon Bay. Such claims, sadly, only make her end all the more tragic.

It was 29 August 1782, the last year of the American Revolutionary War, and the British navy was hard pressed in many quarters. Indeed, the *Royal George* was riding at anchor that day, in a flat calm at Spithead, awaiting final loading and repairs before setting out, as Admiral Richard Kempenfelt's flagship, to try to break the Spanish siege of Gibraltar.

As the vessel was so close to embarkation, all shore leave had been cancelled. The navy had discovered early on that, as action approached, sailors tended to desert, so keeping them aboard was imperative. However, sailors wanted to say farewell to their families and so the captain had allowed on board some 300 women and children (in addition to the 900 crew and marines already aboard). This number also included a good cross-section of the prostitutes, moneylenders and conmen of Portsmouth.

There were also repairs to be done. The *Royal George* had been clad in copper to protect the hull from barnacle growth and this needed to be inspected. A seacock (a tap below the waterline) had to be installed to allow water to be pumped aboard to clean the ship. The carpenters had asked for the vessel to be leant on her side. This was achieved by rolling the guns and some of the ballast all to the port side to make her heel over.

On a flat, calm day this was not an unusual procedure but on this occasion events quickly got out of hand. It didn't help that the sailing master, chief gunner and bo'sun were not on board (contrary to orders), all of whom had a role in overseeing such an operation. When heeling a ship over, it would seem logical to shut the lower portholes on the side closest to the water. But on the morning of 29 August the *Royal George* was also being provisioned and it was found to be much easier to take in provisions through the open gunports now conveniently dipped so close to the water level rather than haul them up on deck. Already the pieces were in place for a disaster.

At around 9 a.m. a cargo vessel known as the *Lark*, variously described as a lighter, a sloop or a fifty-ton cutter, came alongside with the ship's supply of rum. She lashed herself to the port side of the *Royal George* and began unloading her heavy cargo through the gunports, enthusiastically assisted by the crew who noted how much less troublesome the job was made by the ports now being so low in the water. Of course as the rum was loaded on board, the ship began to heel over further. The carpenter noticed the mice running for the upper decks, suggesting that the vessel was taking on water. He went to the officer of the watch and asked for the ship to be righted but received a short and brusque answer.

By now water was clearly entering through the gunports so, just moments later, the carpenter once more requested that the ship be righted. Again he was dismissed, although by now the list was noticeable even to the lieutenant on watch. He ordered the drummer boy to beat out, 'Right ship,' but it was already too late.

Water was now pouring into the gunports and the drummer didn't even have time to fetch his drum before the *Royal George* heeled over on her side and sank in under a minute, taken to the bottom by her rum ration. Exact casualty figures are unknown, as there is no way of accurately gauging the number of civilians or board, but contemporary estimates reckon that only 320 survived from a total of perhaps 1,200, due in part to the sheer speed with which the vessel went down. One child, orphaned by the sinking, survived by clinging to a sheep; nearly all the others drowned. Many of the dead were washed up at Ryde on the Isle of Wight where they were buried in a mass grave on what is now the esplanade.

There was, of course, an inquiry into how so great a ship could sink in calm waters just outside port. Unfortunately for the relatives of those who died, it proved a whitewash. The captain and crew were all exonerated. Instead it was claimed that rotten timbers must have collapsed during the process of heeling her over, causing the hull to stave in.

What did the 'grey ghost' cut in half?

The *Queen Mary* was not designed for war. When she entered service in 1936 she was the most luxurious and fastest liner afloat, taking the Blue Riband for the quickest Atlantic crossing in just under four days. As the pride of the Cunard–White Star Line, she plied Atlantic waters until August 1939 when, having taken to the USA one last consignment of civilians fleeing the war in Europe, she became idle, riding at anchor in New York harbour for six months, before finally being requisitioned as a troopship.

With her sybaritic interior stripped out, her beds replaced with bunks and her hull painted a drab grey, she was the ideal troop carrier. She could carry around 15,000 men at any one time, even managing 16,683 on one trip, and she was so fast – at over 30 knots – that once she was at sea no U-boat could catch her, making an escort unnecessary. From June 1942 the *Queen Mary* was given the task of transporting troops across the North Atlantic where her huge grey form soon acquired the nickname 'the grey ghost' as well as the personal hatred of Hitler, who offered a cash reward and the Iron Cross to any U-boat captain who could sink her.

In the mid-Atlantic, of course, such threats did not bother the *Queen Mary* as she was almost impossible to catch, but when she entered British waters it was a different matter. Now within striking distance of German long-range Condor bombers based in France, and having to reduce speed in coastal waters, she became vulnerable. It was therefore usual for an escort of ships to rendezvous with her off the Irish coast for the final leg of the voyage to Britain.

On 2 October 1942, the *Queen Mary*, bound for Gourock on the Firth of Clyde, met up with three destroyers and the 4,290-ton, C-class, anti-aircraft cruiser, HMS *Curacoa*, off the west coast of Ireland. The *Curacoa* was a rather dated vessel, having entered service in 1918, and it had a top speed of only around 25 knots. It took up station several miles ahead of the *Queen Mary*, fully aware that the huge troopship would overtake it, and its captain, John Boutwood, sent a signal to the *Queen Mary*, indicating that he would 'edge in astern of you'. This was the last clear communication between the vessels. What followed was one of the most tragic naval misunderstandings of the war.

In such dangerous waters where U-boats had already been sighted, the standard procedure was to zigzag, as both the *Queen Mary* and the *Curacoa* now did, but this makes judging relative distances and speeds very difficult. According to the post-war inquiry, neither captain was sure which vessel was meant to be taking the lead in the manoeuvre as, all the while, the huge liner bore down at high speed on the cruiser. In the confusion a fatal mistake was made and the paths of the two ships' zigzags intersected, the *Queen Mary* slicing the *Curacoa* in two at nearly 30 knots. The liner's crew and passengers barely registered a bump.

Sadly this was not the end of the tragedy. The *Queen Mary* was under strict orders not to halt for anything for fear of falling prey to a U-boat. With 11,000 troops on board she could not risk stopping and the crew of the *Curacoa* were left to their fate as the troopship steamed on to the Clyde. The cruiser sank quickly, only 99 members of the 437-man crew managing to escape.

What did Nelson choose *not* to see?

Every commander can be a little blind from time to time, but the one-eyed Nelson had the knack of being blind exactly when he wanted to.

On 2 April 1801, the British fleet under the command of Admiral Sir Hyde Parker and Vice Admiral Horatio Nelson met up with the Danish fleet off the coast of Copenhagen. The Danish were at that time members of the 'Armed Neutrality of the North', a group of nations sworn to prevent the British navy from stopping and searching their vessels during the Napoleonic wars. Britain was, not surprisingly, keen that Denmark should leave this alliance and, having had no luck with diplomacy, thought that the threatening presence of the fleet might help the Danes to see the British point of view.

The plan was simple. Sir Hyde Parker would take his ships north to prevent Russian or Swedish allies from coming to Denmark's aid, whilst Nelson's ships, which included the *Glatton* under the command of one William Bligh, would get in among the Danish fleet at anchor off Copenhagen and sink them. The plan went into effect at 8 a.m. in the morning but did not apparently start well for the British. One ship, the *Agamemnon*, ran aground in shoal waters, trying to turn into the narrow channel where the Danish fleet was positioned, and it was rapidly followed by two others, the *Russell* and the *Bellona*. All were undamaged and all continued firing enthusiastically at the Danes, but being stuck fast they made an easy target.

Nelson, on board the *Elephant*, stood his ground and continued pounding the Danish navy for two hours, aware that a retreat would leave his stranded vessels in dire peril. Sir Hyde Parker, however, was getting nervous and, as overall commander of the expedition, hoisted the signal on his flagship to disengage.

Nelson was certainly not ready to retreat and kept the signal for close action flying from the *Elephant*, acknowledging his colleague's signal but refusing to repeat it. Indeed, only one ship saw the signal to retreat and began withdrawing, bringing on itself even heavier fire, which killed its captain.

According to Colonel Stewart, who was on board the *Elephant*, Nelson then said to him: 'Do you know what's shown on board of the commander-in-chief? No. 39?' Stewart then asked what no. 39 meant and Nelson replied, 'Why, to leave off action. To leave off action! Now damn me if I do.' He then turned to Captain Foley, the master of the *Elephant*, and said: 'You know, Foley, I have only one eye. I have a right to be blind sometimes.' With that, he put his telescope up to his blind eye and pointed it at the commander-in-chief's ship, commenting, 'I really do not see the signal.'

Nelson was proved right to fight on. By the early afternoon the Danish fleet was in tatters. Nineteen of their ships were sunk whilst there were no British losses. The following day Nelson landed in Copenhagen and requested an audience with the crown prince. After a two-hour meeting an indefinite armistice was announced.

Why were there no maidens on the *Idahoe*'s maiden voyage?

For the general concerned with the well-being of his men, there is a great deal more to worry about than enemy fire. Keeping his men healthy and well in often insanitary conditions is no mean feat and soldiers do not always choose to help themselves. It was with this in mind that, on 6 July 1863, as the American Civil War blazed on, special order no. 29 arrived on Lieutenant Colonel George Spalding's desk in Nashville, telling him he was 'directed without loss of time to seize and transport to Louisville all prostitutes found in the city or known to be here'.

The reason for this unusual military manoeuvre was simple,

as the order further describes: 'the presence of venereal disease at this post has elicited the notice of the General Commanding Department who has ordered a pre-emptory remedy.'

So it was that two days later Captain John Newcomb, the proud owner of the newly built steamer *Idahoe*, found his boat chartered by the army and taking on board the unusual cargo of 111 largely irate 'ladies of ill repute', as the local papers liked to call them.

It was not really the sort of work Newcomb had been hoping for from the army, not least because his cargo was so reluctant to leave Nashville and tended towards a playfulness that verged on complete anarchy. Nor was the army particularly helpful, failing to post a proper guard on the ladies and insisting that Newcomb pay for their food, for which he was told to put in a request for reimbursement later.

There was one further, fairly intractable problem. The local newspapers had taken great delight in the story and had warned every city and town on the Cumberland river of the approaching vessel with its undesirable cargo. As a result they all declined to allow Newcomb to land.

After five very difficult days the *Idahoe* finally arrived at its supposed destination, Louisville, and the *Nashville Dispatch* wryly noted that the city would no doubt 'feel proud of such an acquisition to their population'. Needless to say, it did not. The military commander at Louisville flatly refused to take charge of the prostitutes and posted a guard to ensure they didn't disembark, but only after a few of the more daring had already escaped and the more enterprising had won their release by obtaining a writ of habeas corpus. Some of the former were caught and thrown into prison in the city before being 'repatriated' to Nashville by train the next day.

John Newcomb was now in something of a bind with a ship full of prostitutes that no one wanted, at least not officially. In fact he spent much of his time fighting off the young men of Louisville, who kept swimming out to the ship to obtain the unusual services available there, greatly encouraged by the ladies he was trying to rid himself of. For thirteen days the *Idahoe* lay at anchor whilst the newspapers had a field day. The *Cincinatti Daily Gazette* joked that the authorities remained 'too sternly virtuous to allow them to land'.

Eventually the army realised that the situation was impossible and that they were becoming a laughing stock. Newcomb received the order to return to Nashville and on 5 August 1863 the *Idahoe* and its exotic cargo slipped into port, to find awaiting them a large and highly amused crowd. Captain Newcomb, however, was not amused. It took him over two years to be reimbursed the $5,000 costs he had incurred, including $1,000 worth of damage inflicted on his lovely new steamer by its first, unruly passengers.

Who was saved from the Japanese by a coconut?

President John F. Kennedy's tragically short life was almost cut even shorter by an incident when he was simply Lieutenant John F. Kennedy, captain of the torpedo boat PT 109, patrolling off the Solomon Islands.

It was 2 August 1943 and PT 109 was in the Blackett Strait, harrying the regular night-time Japanese convoys of men and munitions bound for the Solomon Islands and New Guinea, known as the 'Tokyo Express'. Fifteen PT boats, each armed with four torpedoes, had set out to attack the convoy but in the ensuing somewhat chaotic action not a single Japanese ship had been sunk. Now most US boats were headed for home, including all those equipped with radar, whilst PT 109 idled in the straits, waiting to see whether any enemy ships reappeared.

In fact one enemy ship was about to do so rather suddenly but, without radar, no one seems to have seen it coming. The first thing that the crew of the PT boat knew about the approach of the Japanese destroyer *Amagiri* was a shout from a lookout that they were in its course, giving them just ten seconds before it hit. Travelling well in excess of 20 knots, the destroyer simply cut the little vessel in half, leaving it to sink. Two of Kennedy's crew died in the immediate aftermath of the attack and the other eleven were thrown into a sea alight with burning fuel oil.

For the next four hours the survivors who could swim pushed a piece of wreckage, bearing those who couldn't, the six kilometres to the nearest land, a tiny, foodless and waterless islet called Plum Pudding Island. Kennedy, who had swum for Harvard, towed one of his badly burnt crew all the way by clamping the strap of the injured man's lifejacket in his teeth. Plum Pudding Island could only be a temporary refuge as they were sitting ducks there, so Kennedy swam another four kilometres until he found an island with coconut palms and fresh water. He then led his men to its relative safety.

On Olosana Island the men dug in and waited for rescue. Fortunately the destruction of PT 109 had been noticed by an Australian coastwatcher who had a hidden observation post on an island on which over 10,000 Japanese soldiers were billeted. Unable to leave his post, he recruited two locals, Buiku Gasa and Eroni Kumana, to search the area in a dugout posing as fishermen.

It was six days later that Gasa and Kumana finally made contact with the missing crew. Their dugout was nowhere near large enough to evacuate them so they offered to take a message instead. The problem was that no one had any paper on them, nor was there apparently anything suitable on the small island. After some head-scratching, Gasa suggested carving the message on the husk of a coconut. Kennedy agreed, writing: 'NAURO ISL COMMANDER . . . NATIVE KNOWS POSIT . . . HE CAN PILOT . . . 11 ALIVE NEED SMALL BOAT . . . KENNEDY.'

The local men carried this vital rescue coconut through sixty kilometres of Japanese-controlled waters to the nearest Allied base. PT 157 was then dispatched and the survivors rescued.

In 1961, to show there were no hard feelings, Kennedy invited the captain of the *Amagiri* to his inauguration, at which the Japanese officer is reported to have politely apologised for deliberately running down the PT boat. The liberating coconut also remained close to Kennedy, spending its White House years on his desk in the Oval Office. It now has pride of place in the John F. Kennedy Library in Boston.

How did a flag sink a submarine?

Mistaken identity is often the cause of tragedy in wartime but there can be few more unfortunate incidents than the sinking of the British submarine HMS J6.

The advent of large-scale submarine warfare in the First World War brought a new game of deception into play. Rather unsportingly, the German U-boats had taken to torpedoing shipping without warning, but if the U-boats weren't going to announce their presence before sinking merchantmen (thus allowing the crew to abandon ship), the British merchantmen would have to fight back.

The answer that the navy came up with were Q ships – vessels that looked for all the world like ordinary merchantmen but which contained hidden weaponry. These vessels would patrol the sea looking for surfaced U-boats – and it should be noted that these early submarines had to spend a great deal of their time on the surface. When they came across one, the U-boat would take no notice – it was just a merchant ship – giving the crew of the Q ship time to unleash their hidden weapons on the hapless Germans and sink them.

So it was that on 15 October 1918 the former schooner *Cymric*, now a Q ship, was patrolling the North Sea off the Northumberland coast near Blyth. It had been a frustrating day for the crew who had already encountered two submarines, only to discover that they were British. Now, at 4 p.m., however, as they closed in on another submarine, the lookout was convinced that they had a target – the U6 – its number clearly painted on the conning tower in large letters.

Quite separately that day, the British J-class submarine J6 had been patrolling these same waters and was, at 4 p.m., surfaced just on the edge of a fog bank, when the *Cymric* hove into view. As it was a British vessel, the crew of the J6 took no notice despite the fact that the ship was bearing down sharply on them. They did take notice the next moment, however, when, with a flourish, the *Cymric* unfurled a naval white ensign – similar to the one hanging limply down the side of the J6's conning tower. Moments later the Q ship opened fire. The signalman on the J6 tried desperately to hoist a recognition signal but was killed by a shell. The captain of the J6 manoeuvred his stricken craft into the fog bank, hoping to escape, but the damage had already been done. The crew of the *Cymric* noted with puzzlement the 'help' signal flashing through the fog but only realised what had happened when they began pulling submariners from the water with 'HMS J6' headbands on their caps.

Fourteen men, just under half the crew, on the J6 died in the attack but the court of inquiry laid no blame on the captain of the *Cymric*. Tragically, the white ensign attached to the submarine had hung down right next to the 'J' painted on the conning tower, making it appear like a 'U'. Even when the signalman had frantically waved the ensign, the Q ship crew assumed that this was a ruse – and one that had been used before. The court ruled that the sinking was a 'hazard of war'. When the *Cymric*'s captain, Lieutenant Commander Geoffrey Warburton, left the inquiry room, the surviving crew of the J6 stood to salute him.

Which Greek idea helped the Dutch defeat the Spanish?

During the Eighty Years War the city of Breda in the southern part of the Netherlands suffered more than most. In 1581, Spanish troops had taken the city by surprise, having bribed a sentry to open the castle gates to them. With the castle in enemy hands, the people of Breda offered to surrender in return for their city not being sacked, but a massacre ensued in which some 584 citizens lost their lives.

These events made Breda something of an icon for the Dutch

and it became a matter of national pride in the House of Orange to retake it. The question was, how?

The solution was just about as old as a military tactic gets: hide your soldiers inside an apparently innocent object and wait for it to be taken inside your enemy's stronghold. It had worked for the Achaeans outside Troy and one Dutch sailor, Adriaen van Bergen, believed it would work again. He approached Prince Maurice of Nassau with an idea. Van Bergen owned a peat barge that made regular trips into the castle, taking fuel for the garrison, which was now an Italian unit under the command of Odoardo Lanzavecchia. His boat, being full of muddy, stinking peat, was never checked and hence made the ideal vessel in which to smuggle soldiers.

Maurice liked the idea and, at 11 a.m. on 25 February 1590, sixty-eight hand-picked men, under the command of the future governor of Breda, Charles de Héraugières, were sent to the river to find van Bergen and secrete themselves on his boat. Van Bergen, however, was nowhere to be seen and it was only after hours of searching that he was finally tracked down. Although he claimed to have overslept, he was clearly worried that the plan had been uncovered. By then it was too late to sail. He offered to be there the following night but seems to have lost his nerve and sent his two nephews instead.

Under their command, the sixty-eight men, three officers and de Héraugières were huddled in the hold of the barge and covered in peat before the boat set sail for a long, cold and wet journey against the wind to Breda. It had been decided to make the whole voyage undercover so as not to arouse suspicion, even though this meant the men would not be able to move or eat until they arrived. After the men had spent four days in cramped conditions in the hold when the boat was stationary, due to ice blocking the river, it was agreed to put in at night and let them out briefly.

The soldiers spent a further two days aboard, covered in peat, before the barge reached the watergate of the castle. A cursory inspection failed to discover them but disaster nearly struck at the last minute when the barge was holed while mooring up, and icy water began pouring into the vessel, requiring the hidden cargo to pump for dear life. The Italian garrison now unwittingly came to the aid of their nemesis, tying the barge fast to the quay above the line of the damage.

That night the men and officers of what is known in Dutch history as the Turfschip van Breda stole out of their barge and took the castle, much to the dismay of the sleeping garrison. With the main city defences now in their hands, they were able to signal to Maurice of Nassau, whose army was waiting outside. The gates were opened and Breda fell to the Dutch.

What was Tom Thumb's big mistake?

By October 1941 it was becoming increasingly clear to British commanders that Japan was likely to enter the war and so a naval force was prepared for the protection of the British possession of Singapore. It was to be an impressive little fleet, consisting of the brand-new battleship *Prince of Wales* with its ten fourteen-inch guns, the famous cruiser *Repulse*, which had battle honours dating back to the First World War, the aircraft carrier *Indomitable*, and an escort of destroyers. The command was given to Admiral Sir Thomas Philips, known as 'Tom Thumb'. He was highly regarded by the navy, although this regard relied on dim memories of the last time he was in combat, which was twenty-four years earlier, in 1917.

The world and warfare had changed somewhat since then and, in particular, the era of the big battleship was giving way to the age of the aircraft. Planes that had been little more than bags of sticks and canvas in 1917 had been replaced by fast effective fighters and bombers, but Tom Thumb still believed that these were irrelevant against the mighty ships of the British navy.

So Force Z, as it was known, set sail, although without the aircraft carrier *Indomitable*, which had run aground in the West Indies. The *Hermes* would have been available to replace her but it was not thought vital that Force Z should have extensive air cover – after all, what could Japanese planes do against battleships? – so they left without her.

Force Z arrived off Singapore on 2 December 1941, five days before Pearl Harbor. Feeling reasonably invulnerable, the *Repulse* was detached from the force to go to Australia to see whether any of their ships might like to join the flotilla. By then it was 5 December and the Japanese force for the invasion of Malaya had already set sail – although no one else had noticed. The next day it was finally spotted and the *Repulse* was told to turn back sharpish.

On the night of 7 December the Japanese force began invading Malaya from the coast and the Thai border. The RAF were soon driven back, leaving no air cover save for an ageing squadron of Brewster Buffaloes. Undaunted, Tom Thumb set sail on 8 December to counter the invasion with Force Z but with no real air cover. The following day his fleet was spotted by a Japanese submarine and the element of surprise was lost. Coming under increasing attack from the air, Philips was forced to abort the mission and turn tail that evening. Just after midnight he received a new report of landings back in the direction in which he was now steaming and he decided to attack there, although the reports turned out to be false. By now no one knew where Tom Thumb was, as he was operating under radio silence, although at least this meant that the Japanese couldn't find him either.

Finally at 11 a.m. the next morning a Japanese reconnaissance plane did spot the flotilla and a huge aerial attack was set in motion. Tom Thumb's fleet, which he considered impregnable to air attack, was now savaged by fifty-one torpedo bombers and thirty-four bombers. The *Repulse* was torpedoed in the steering compartment, jamming its rudder hard over, which forced it to steam in a circle until it was finally sunk at 12.35 p.m. The brand-new *Prince of Wales* was by now zigzagging desperately, having been hit twice, but at 1.10 a bomb pierced the deck and exploded in the casualty station below, blowing a huge hole in the hull. Philips gave the order to abandon ship and ten minutes later the

Prince of Wales capsized and sank. In all, 840 men, including Tom Thumb, lost their lives, demonstrating that in modern warfare ruling the waves was no longer enough.

Why did Admiral Price end it all?

The story of Rear Admiral David Price is one of the sadder episodes in British naval history and it says as much about the structural failures of the navy as it does about the man himself.

Price had entered the navy in 1801 and quickly distinguished himself in battle. He was present at the Battle of Copenhagen, was twice captured and released by the Danes, and was severely injured during one of his many successful raids harrying French shipping out of Barfleur. After a year-long recovery, further adventures beckoned off the North American coast where he was again injured in operations at New Orleans, before returning to a Mediterranean command that so impressed the Greek government that they awarded him the Order of the Redeemer of Greece.

But the Royal Navy of the 1840s did not manage its captains well. With no further immediate work for Price, he was returned to England and placed on shore leave at half-pay. For six years he waited before another land-based command arose as superintendent of Sheerness docks. Indeed, it was 1853 before Price, now thoroughly out of practice, was suddenly given command of the Pacific fleet, just before the outbreak of the Crimean War.

The command structure that Price found in the Pacific was labyrinthine and cumbersome, and his French counterparts proved difficult to work with. In July 1854, the British and French fleets met at Honolulu to search for the Russian frigate *Aurora*, which was reported to be at sea. They finally tracked it down on the other side of the Pacific, laid up at Petropavlovsk on the Russian peninsula of Kamchatka. It was immediately decided to attack Petropavlovsk although Price was clearly nervous about engaging substantial shore batteries and anxious for the safety of his men. After his years of inaction – fearing a return to the 'half-pay' list, and now faced with the huge responsibility of taking the British (and French) Pacific squadrons into a battle he was unsure he could win – he cracked under the pressure. On the evening of 30 August, the day of the proposed attack, David Price retired to his cabin and shot himself.

In a final cruel twist of fate, the bullet missed his heart and entered his lung, leaving him to die a slow and painful death. During this time the officers of the squadron, and the French admiral, were summoned to see him one by one so that Price could personally apologise to them, telling them that he had acted as he had because he could not bear the thought that many of them would lose their lives in the coming engagement. Price died later that day and the command passed to Captain Sir Frederick Nicolson of HMS *Pique*, who ordered the attack for 1 September. As Price had feared, it proved a disaster, and the French and British were forced to withdraw with five times as many casualties as the Russians. As they sailed away, they left behind the body of David Price, who had been buried on the day of the attack beneath a tree on the shore, his initials carved in the bark above to mark his last resting place.

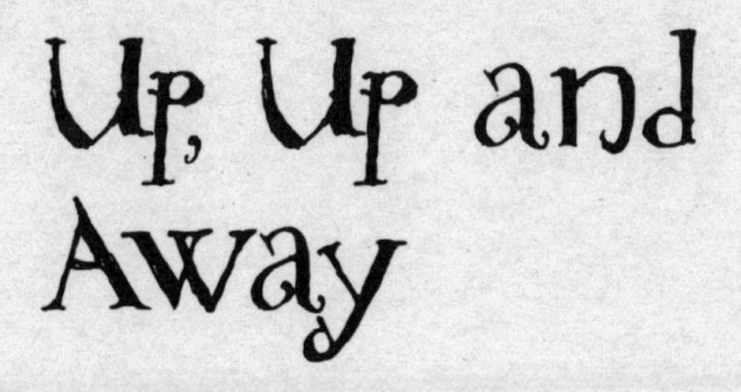

Up, Up and Away

Heavier-than-air flying machines are impossible.

William Thomson, Lord Kelvin, President of the Royal Society (1895)

How did Captain Strange wreck his cockpit?

The First World War was the experimental proving ground of aerial combat. The first powered flight had only taken place in 1903 yet by 1914 aeroplanes were already finding a wartime role, initially as scouts. Nevertheless, General Haig – who would, rather worryingly, become commander-in-chief of the British Expeditionary Force in 1915 – commented: 'I hope none of you gentlemen is so foolish as to think that aeroplanes will be able to be usefully employed for reconnaissance in the air. There is only one way for a commander to get information by reconnaissance and that is by the use of cavalry.'

Fortunately the nascent Royal Flying Corps did not take his words to heart and continued the unequal struggle – and struggle it was, thanks in no small part to the machines they were expected to fly. At the start of the war no one really knew what a fighter plane, or indeed a bomber, should look like. Everyone agreed that guns would be a good idea but where do you put them? If you put them in front of the pilot, they'd turn the propeller to matchwood when fired. If you put them to one side, the pilot couldn't really see where he was aiming. There was an answer of course (see page 227) but it wasn't the one chosen for the Martinsyde S1 biplane scout.

The S1 wasn't a very good plane when all was said and done; indeed, it was in use on the Western Front for only six months before being relegated, first to home defence and then training. The main problem with the S1 was that its machine-gun was placed on top of the upper wing, directly above the pilot. He could fire this gun from his seat and it didn't splinter his propeller, which was helpful, but if it jammed or ran out of ammunition, to reload the pilot had to stand up on his seat, clamping the joystick between his knees to keep the plane on course. This proved hazardous, as the splendid Lieutenant Louis A. Strange would discover.

On 10 May 1915, Strange was locked in combat with a German

Aviatik, which soon climbed out of range, but not before Strange had loosed off all forty-six rounds in his Lewis gun's magazine. This left him in a tricky situation. The Aviatik was coming back towards him but Strange had no ammo left, so, careless of life or limb, he decided to reload. He unstrapped himself and stood up, controlling the plane with the joystick held between his knees, but the magazine was jammed. Flying a plane with your knees is no easy feat, particularly when tugging at a machine-gun, and in the process his plane stalled. At this point Strange became suddenly very pleased that the magazine was jammed as it was all he was holding on to when his plane flipped over. He was now upside down, hanging out of his plane, holding on only by the Lewis gun, and things did not look good. Indeed, so sure was his opponent that Strange's war was over that he turned tail and flew away without finishing him off.

Strange was made of sterner stuff, however, and he managed to climb back into the cockpit, still upside down, and flip his plane back the right way up, crashing down into its wicker seat in the process with such force that it splintered, and smashing some of the controls. Somehow he managed to wrestle his plane back to base, where he made a safe landing. At the aerodrome his commanding officer quizzed him on how he had managed to destroy the cockpit of an otherwise intact aircraft. His reply is not recorded.

Who took a plane but swam for home?

There are many tales of the unusual behaviour of General Ioannis Metaxas, the ruler of Greece (although he styled himself 'First Peasant') under the '4th August regime', which lasted from August 1936 until his death in 1941. Some of these have as much to do with a dislike of his authoritarian rule as they do with the truth, but one in particular does seem to be well attested and must somehow have escaped the strict censorship of the period.

When Metaxas was inspecting a military airbase, as was his

wont, he was shown around a new seaplane that rather took his fancy. Being a qualified pilot himself, he asked whether he might take the plane up for a spin. Few wishing to disappoint their leader, the trip was agreed. Metaxas took off from the base's harbour and made a few circles of the installation before radioing the tower that he was coming in to land.

It was as he lined up the plane for a final approach to the runway that the air-traffic controller, overcoming his fear of the general, radioed to say that perhaps, as the aircraft was a seaplane, he might have more success landing it on the water rather than on the somewhat unforgiving concrete runway.

Fortunately Metaxas was prepared to admit his mistake and aborted the landing, coming round again and finally putting the machine down perfectly in the still waters of the harbour. Aware of what a fool, and potentially what a dead fool, he might have looked if he had crashed the seaplane on dry land, before leaving the cockpit he radioed the air-traffic controller to thank him for saving his blushes.

Happy that he had done the decent thing, he then opened the cockpit door and jumped down – straight into the sea.

Who had the first bird's-eye view?

The Battle of Fleurus in the French revolutionary wars marked the introduction of a whole new type of technology to warfare, which proved to be a stunning, if unexpected, success.

In June 1794, the 70,000-strong French army of the Sambre-Meuse, under the command of Jean-Baptiste Jourdan, squared up to the Austrian and Netherlands army of 52,000 men, under the command of Prince Frederick Josias of Saxe-Coburg-Saalfeld. The prince had arrived to relieve the besieged garrison of Charleroi just in time to witness its surrender to the French and he immediately set about counter-attacking. On 26 June he split his army into five columns and advanced on the enemy lines.

What happened next caused some considerable confusion

among his troops. From behind the massing lines of French infantry, a large shape began to rise up into the sky – a huge balloon. The Austrian troops were unsure what this presaged and fired wildly at the monster, which some said proved that France did indeed have a pact with 'the Evil One'.

Fortunately for Captain Coutel, an *aérostier* in the brand-new aeronautic corps of the French army, as well as for the adjutants and general accompanying him in the basket, the terrified Austrians proved poor shots. Before they could bring their guns accurately to bear on the balloon, it had sailed far above the range of their muskets and cannons.

This magnificent ascent was the first time an aircraft of any type had been used in battle and *L'Entreprenant*, as she was known, proved invaluable. Twice during the day Coutel ascended some 440 yards on a tether to survey the battlefield and report back on Austrian and Dutch troop movements, staying aloft for four hours at a time and relaying his findings through a series of flag signals. A description of this first reconnaissance flight in military history from 1822 described the serene scene: 'Having arrived at the intended height, the observers, remote from danger, and undisturbed, viewed all the evolutions of the enemy, and, from a peaceful region of the air, commanded a distinct and comprehensive prospect of the two formidable armies engaged in the work of death.'

The advantage given to General Jourdan by being able to see the battle unfolding from the air, like the pieces on a wargaming board, was incalculable, particularly considering that he had to manoeuvre 70,000 men around the field. The result was a stunning victory for the French and full Allied withdrawal from Belgium.

How did a laundry trip give the game away?

Hellmuth Reinberger was an important man in the German command system in January 1940, as he held the key to the imminent conquest of Europe. Thanks to a good dinner, the unexpected offer of a lift and a series of wholly farcical events, he would earn the personal animosity of the Führer and change the course of the opening stages of the war.

Reinberger, a major in the parachute division, had been entrusted with the plans for the invasion of Holland and Belgium when, on 9 January 1940, he was summoned to Cologne to discuss their imminent implementation. That evening he was in the officers' mess in Münster, complaining to his old friend Major Erich Hoenmanns about the long and tedious train journey he would have to take in the morning, when Hoenmanns, the commandant of the nearby Loddenheide airfield, had an idea. He needed to get some more flying hours in his logbook so he was considering a trip home to Cologne to see his wife and drop off his dirty laundry. Perhaps Major Reinberger would like a lift? It was entirely against security regulations, as Reinberger had the battle plans on him, but it would be quick and convenient. What could possibly go wrong?

So the next morning, after a convivial night in the bar, the two men drove out to Loddenheide and climbed aboard a Messerschmitt Bf108 trainer. Not long after take-off, the weather began to close in and blow the little plane off course. Then the engine cut out, possibly because Hoenmanns, who had only ever flown this type of plane once before, accidentally switched off the fuel supply. A crash landing looked likely but Hoenmanns managed to bring the plane down successfully. He, Reinberger and the secret plans found themselves in a snow-covered thicket. This seemed like a lucky escape until they consulted their map and realised they were near Mechelen-sur-Meuse in Allied-controlled Belgium and holding the plans for the invasion of that very country.

Reinberger thought fast and immediately decided to set fire to the plans, only to discover that, unusually, neither he nor Hoenmanns smoked so they had no matches. Flagging down a passing and no doubt bemused labourer, they managed to beg some matches and started burning the documents just as a Belgian patrol appeared.

Astonishingly the Belgian soldiers didn't seem to register the furious and furtive activity and Reinberger was able to tuck the papers (the vast majority of which he had failed to destroy) under his arm before he was marched off for interrogation. There another stroke of luck befell him as he was left unsupervised in a room with a lit stove, into which he immediately stuffed the battle plans. At this point his luck ran out. The arresting officer returned and noticed that something was missing. Searching around, he found the charred (but readable) papers in the stove and removed them. The Allies now had the German invasion plans.

Hitler was furious, as might be expected, and a number of high-ranking officers were fired for no apparent reason. Reinberger and Hoenmanns were both sentenced to death *in absentia* but, fortunately for them, remained Allied prisoners of war in Canada until the end of hostilities.

What happened to Zeppelin L-19?

As the Austrians had found to their cost in 1849 (see page 192), one of the most important aspects of aerial bombing is making sure your bombs fall on the right target. By the First World War, this required that the pilots and crew of aircraft knew where they were and where they were going, which wasn't always the case.

The first civilian bombing raids of the war were carried out by the Zeppelin airships, which, though very large and highly flammable (they were filled with hydrogen gas), could fly higher than any British fighter plane and could thus bomb with impunity – provided they could find their target. This was easier said than done, however,

The first problem faced by the nine-Zeppelin raid that set out from Germany on 31 January 1916 was that their commander's geography was not that good. Their orders from the legendary Korvettenkapitän Peter Strasser were to bomb the Midlands or the southern area, particularly Liverpool – which showed a hazy understanding of where Liverpool actually was.

So the mission set out in a confused state, made worse by fog in the Channel and high winds that blew the lightweight machines off course. Nevertheless, eight of the Zeppelins returned intact to report their successes. Amongst them, L-21 reported a successful raid on Liverpool, although it had actually bombed Birmingham; L-16 reported bombing Great Yarmouth, when in fact it had hit Swaffham; and L-13 claimed to have terrorised Manchester, when it had actually grazed Scunthorpe.

It was not exactly what had been planned but no doubt bombing anywhere in England at this date had the desired effect of making the British feel vulnerable, so the mission could at some level be considered a success. That is unless you were in the crew of Zeppelin L-19. The captain of L-19, Odo Loewe, had sent a message to base confirming he was bombing Liverpool although eyewitneses say he was actually over Worcestershire at the time. He then dropped some bombs on Wednesbury, which he thought was Sheffield, before heading east over the Norfolk coast. At this point, his radio went quiet.

For nine hours from the last message there was silence. German naval units were scrambled to search for the missing airship but, before they could make contact, Loewe finally radioed in to say he was safe over the German island of Borkum and limping slowly home after three of his four engines had failed. Tragically for Loewe and his crew, his knowledge of the European coast was no better than his knowledge of England. He was actually over Dutch waters and as he descended – in the belief that he was on friendly ground – the Dutch opened fire. Loewe managed to turn his crippled airship around and head out over the North Sea but, either due to the failure of his last engine or damage sustained from the Dutch attack, the L-19 crashed into the icy waters.

Loewe and his crew were next spotted by an English trawler, the *King Stephen*, which stopped to talk to the men as they sat huddled in a shelter on the top of the partially submerged gas envelope. They asked to be taken aboard but the trawler captain refused, claiming he feared being taken hostage, and having his ship commandeered and sailed to Germany. He did, however, promise to tell any patrol he met of their whereabouts.

That was the last time anyone saw the L-19, Odo Loewe or his crew. It is assumed that the airship finally sank a few hours later, taking the entire crew to a watery grave. All that survived to tell of the tragedy was a message in a bottle, written by Captain Loewe just before the end. It read:

> With 15 men on the top platform and backbone girder of the L19, floating without gondolas in approximately 3 degrees East longitude, I am attempting to send a last report. Engine trouble three times repeated, a light head wind on the return journey delayed our return and, in the mist, carried us over Holland where I was received with heavy rifle-fire. The ship became heavy and simultaneously three engines failed. February 2nd., towards 1 p.m., will apparently be our last hour.
>
> Loewe

How did the British win the Battle of the Beams?

By 1940, German bombers had improved their navigation considerably after the rather haphazard efforts of the First World War (see page 102). Just how they were managing to find their targets in England, regardless of weather, was a subject that particularly vexed Dr Reginald V. Jones of the Royal Aircraft Establishment, who had been seconded to the Air Ministry's Intelligence section. His job was to identify new German technologies and counter them. He had worked out that the Germans were using a system of radio navigation beams. Two focussed beams would be transmitted from separate base stations, which crossed over the intended target. The bombers would fly down one beam and, when they started receiving the other, they knew they were over the target and could drop their bombs.

Having discovered the trick behind the early version of this system, known as *Knickebein* (crooked leg), Jones could send jamming signals to throw the bombers off course, but the Germans soon became wise to this and changed the system. So began the 'Battle of the Beams'.

Sometime in 1940, the whole *Knickebein* system was supplemented by the splendidly named and much more accurate *X-Gerät* (X-gadget), which operated at frequencies unknown to the British, making Jones desperate to discover how it worked. Following a raid on the Midlands on 5 November, he had a stroke of luck. One of the Heinkel He111 bombers fitted with the *X-Gerät* system developed a faulty compass and, thinking it was over France, was persuaded to land on the beach at Bridport in Dorset. A coastal defence army officer immediately posted guards around this precious find and ordered the sentries to prevent anyone from approaching the machine, adding, 'I don't care if even an admiral comes along. You are not to allow him near it.'

But here Jones was unfortunate. The plane was resting between the high- and low-tide marks and the tide was rapidly coming in. It was clear to everyone that the plane would be inundated if it wasn't relocated, but the sentries, faithful to their orders, refused all offers of help to move the machine. Instead they watched as it disappeared beneath the waves. The following day the aircraft was salvaged but the delicate *X-Gerät* system had been badly corroded by the salt water. Jones later reported that if he had been able to recover the equipment intact, he could have introduced countermeasures within days. Eight days later, Coventry was bombed.

What happened when the American balloon went up?

The Spanish-American War of 1898 was a brief and now largely forgotten conflict in which the USA sought to support Cuba's calls for independence from Spain – and at the same time increase their influence in the Spanish-speaking world at the expense of Spain's fast-diminishing empire. America declared war on Spain after the mysterious sinking of the US battleship *Maine*, which blew up in Havana harbour, although to this day no one quite knows whether the explosion was caused by a mine or a fire in one of the ship's coal bunkers.

Whatever the cause, it was a good enough reason for war, at least in the minds of US newspaper owners like William Randolph Hearst. He began a campaign of 'yellow journalism', accusing the Spanish authorities of terrible atrocities in their overseas dominions. On 23 April, war was duly declared and US troops headed for Cuba in support of the Cuban independence movement.

The fighting on the island reached a climax at the Battle of San Juan Hill on 1 July. With 12,000 US troops hacking their way through thick jungle, and the Spanish dug in on the heights, reconnaissance was obviously vital but the method chosen by the US signals corps seemed to many of the war correspondents present to be rather peculiar. They were employing a tethered hot-air balloon, manned by one Lieutenant Colonel Derby, to spot enemy positions from their own front line.

The use of balloons for reconnaissance was a tried and tested tactic and a useful one at that, but not in all situations. Lieutenant Colonel Derby, floating high above the jungle, had put himself in a rather precarious one. Not only could he not see the enemy but he couldn't see his own men to report back to either. The Spanish, however, had no such trouble. Although they had been previously uncertain as to which way the American attack could come, they could now clearly see the huge balloon bobbing over the trees towards them and rightly surmised that the US troops were beneath it. They concentrated their fire in that direction, to lethal effect.

Richard Harding Davis, in his *Notes of a War Correspondent*, described the scene:

> The observation balloon hastened the end. It came blundering down the trail, and stopped the advance of the First and Tenth

> cavalry, and was sent up directly over the heads of our men to observe what should have been observed a week before by scouts and reconnoitring parties . . . a balloon on the advance line, and only fifty feet above the tops of the trees, was merely an invitation to the enemy to kill everything beneath it. And the enemy responded to the invitation. A Spaniard might question if he could hit a man, or a number of men, hidden in the bushes, but had no doubt at all as to his ability to hit a mammoth glistening ball only six hundred yards distant, and so all the trenches fired at it at once, and the men of the First and Tenth, packed together directly behind it, received the full force of the bullets.

The result was carnage but Lieutenant Colonel Derby doggedly did his duty until some well-aimed shrapnel bursts finally brought down his craft. Richard Harding Davis heard his report:

> Captain Howse, of General Sumner's staff, rode down the trail to learn what had delayed the First and Tenth, and was hailed by Colonel Derby, who was just descending from the shattered balloon.
>
> 'I saw men up there on these hills,' Colonel Derby shouted. 'They are firing at our troops.' That was the part of the information contributed by the balloon. Captain Howse's reply is lost to history.

What did the raven say to Augustus?

Not all classical authors can be relied upon to give wholly accurate information on their subjects, partly because many wrote at a great distance in time or space from the events they recorded, but also because the concept of accurate history was then very different. Thus the *Saturnalia* by Ambrosius Theodosius Macrobius, a collection of discussions that supposedly took place over one Saturnalia – a public holiday – should be taken with a pinch of salt, not least when he's describing events that occurred over 400 years earlier.

In one of these incidents he tells a tale about the first emperor Augustus, which, if not provable in its detail, gives an insight into the tense situation at the end of the Roman Civil War and the lengths that some Romans would go to to ensure they emerged on the winning side.

Macrobius tells us that Augustus – on his triumphant return from the Battle of Actium, where he had defeated the fleets of Mark Antony and Cleopatra – was welcomed back into Rome. Among the well-wishers who thronged around him was a man with a raven, which he had trained to say, 'Greetings to Caesar, our victorious commander.' Augustus was delighted with this novelty, which, apart from anything else, showed an apparent degree of loyalty, as it would have taken the man some time to train the bird to say this. He gave him the princely sum of 20,000 sesterces for the raven's prowess and the man left happy.

His happiness was brief. The bird trainer had a business partner, who, it seems, never received his half of the money, so he decided to take his revenge. He informed Augustus that his partner had another raven and that he should demand to see it. The now rather nervous raven trainer and his other bird were duly hauled before the emperor and all waited with bated breath for the raven to 'speak'. With absolutely no loyalty to its owner, the bird squawked, 'Greetings to Antony, our victorious commander.'

Fortunately for both men, Augustus saw the funny side and let them both go, only insisting that they share the money between them as they had originally agreed. There is no record of the fate of the two ravens.

The Dogs of War

Unceasingly they had drummed into them the utterance of *The Times*: 'You are lions led by pack-asses.'

Francisque Sarcey, *Paris during the Siege* (1871), of French troops defeated by Prussians

What use is an exploding dog?

The Great Patriotic War, as the Russians refer to the Second World War, required extraordinary sacrifices, not only from the Soviet people themselves but also from their animals. In particular, in the autumn of 1941 during the defence of Moscow, the Russian army began, long before the Japanese had the idea, to unleash its own kamikaze weapon in the form of mine dogs. The idea was simple, if a shade disturbing for any animal lovers watching.

According to a report compiled by the US Department of the Army for the Secretary of the Army, the Russians had trained a number of medium-sized dogs to run under tanks by hiding their food in the tracks. In battle conditions, these dogs, which were kept hungry, were fitted with a canvas jacket containing four pouches holding between ten and twelve kilograms of high-explosive demolition charges. The explosive was attached to an igniter that was initiated by a fifteen-centimetre-long, spring-loaded spindle standing upright on the animal's back, which acted as a trigger. When the hapless animal crawled under a German tank in search of food, the spindle was depressed and the igniter fired, detonating the charge and destroying the tank (and the dog).

Sadly for the Soviet army, but fortunately for the dogs, the system proved rather unreliable. There are no firm records for the number of 'kills' achieved by the mine dogs and, perhaps not surprisingly, Russian and German accounts of their success differ somewhat. We do know that the advent of the kamikaze canine made the battlefield a considerably more dangerous place for any dog to be as the Germans took to shooting any and every animal that strayed into their path, just in case.

German sources also claim that the dogs proved completely ineffective anyway as the thundering approach of panzers rather put them off their lunch and hence reduced their inclination to clamber under the approaching tanks. Indeed, they contend that not a single German tank was ever destroyed by the weapon.

Soviet sources counter that, in the huge 1943 Battle of Kursk, sixteen dogs were successfully deployed, destroying twelve tanks between them. Even if this were the case, the Soviet High Command did not believe that this tactic could turn the tide of war and the dogs soon disappeared from the battlefields. US reports suggest that this might be because the panicked animals, finding themselves in the paths of belligerent tanks, tended to run for cover beneath their own vehicles, blowing up more Soviet than German tanks in the process.

What did Prince Rupert do with his Boy?

Warfare involves a combination of skill and fortune but it is all too easy for an army that suddenly finds itself on the losing side to assume that its enemy has some unknown and unfair advantage that has turned the tide.

During the English Civil War the successes of the Royalist Prince Rupert of the Rhine particularly exercised the minds of Parliamentarians. As he was a hated enemy, it seemed impossible, and frankly unpatriotic, to put his victories down to expertise or even luck, so in an atmosphere charged with Puritanical fervour the news spread around the troops that Prince Rupert's key advantage was the diabolical powers he received from his pet dog, Boy. As one writer put it: 'Is not this dog no dog, but a witch and a sorceress and an Enemy to parliament?'

In an era when the devil was widely believed to act in person in the world, and send demons and familiars to work his will, the idea of a prince having a diabolical dog was not as peculiar as it sounds today. If the devil disguised himself as a black poodle for Dr Faustus, why shouldn't he disguise himself as a white one for Prince Rupert?

So the white poodle always at the prince's side took on demonic proportions in the minds of the Parliamentarian pamphlet writers. It was said that the animal was dagger-proof and could catch musket balls in its teeth. When not performing these stunts it was able to talk to its master in a dialect that apparently was not unlike Hebrew. It could also sniff out buried treasure should the need arise.

More salaciously it was reported in one pamphlet that the prince had trained the animal to perform unspecified sexual services on him and that they lay 'perpetually in one bed, sometimes the Prince upon the dog, and sometimes the dog upon the Prince; and what this may in time produce, none but the close committee can tell'.

Another pamphlet from 1642 came up with another fanciful explanation of the dog's true identity:

> I have kept a very strict eye upon this dogge, whom I cannot conclude to be a very downright divell, but some Lapland ladye, once by nature a handsome white ladye, but now by art a handsome white dogge. They have many times attempted to destroy it by poyson and extempore prayer, but they hurt him no more than the plague plaister did Mr Pym.

Boy's end came at the Battle of Marston Moor, on 2 July 1644. Prince Rupert had left the animal in the care of servants but it had broken loose and faithfully followed its master into battle. Exactly what happened next is uncertain but on the following day Boy's body was found among the dead – probably trampled to death by the horses. The Parliamentarian pamphleteers had a field day, noting that, with the death of the 'accursed dogge', the fortunes of Prince Rupert had changed and parliament was in the ascendancy. Some also recorded that the brave soldier who killed Boy must have been a master of necromancy to overcome this dagger-proof, bullet-catching demon.

How did Mellish do his donkey work?

Henry Francis Mellish was one of those nineteenth-century British soldiers who was so much larger than life that it is surprising that they could find a uniform to fit him. Mellish was an English gentleman through and through – a personal friend of the Prince Regent (not that that made anyone necessarily a gentleman), a captain in the 10th Hussars and ADC to Sir Ronald Ferguson, one of Wellington's most distinguished generals during the Peninsular War.

During this campaign Mellish happened to be captured, something that seemed to bother neither the captain nor his commanding officer – on hearing the news Wellington allegedly commented that the enemy 'wouldn't keep him long'. And so it proved, when Mellish appeared again the next day, having escaped from his captors on the back of a donkey.

For a Hussar a donkey was scarcely a suitable mount and Mellish was immediately teased that his animal wasn't worth £5. He replied that he would soon make it worth £35 and, with his usual reckless aplomb, he promptly turned the beast around and trotted towards the enemy positions. In a few short paces the poor creature was shot dead from under him whereupon the captain scrambled back to his own lines to claim the £35 government bounty for the loss of one's mount in battle.

What use is a pig against an elephant?

The war elephant was the tank of the ancient world – a huge beast whose presence alone on the battlefield was enough to unnerve the Romans during their war with Hannibal. Their size and momentum made them very good at breaking up the formal infantry formations of the day and their intelligence made them reasonably controllable. But they did have weaknesses.

Elephants are not naturally terribly warlike and will generally settle for a quiet life if at all possible. For example, the Roman general Scipio Africanus found that he could take the sting out of an elephant charge simply by opening up avenues between his troops – down which the elephants would naturally run in preference to crashing into his heavily armoured lines of soldiers.

Once the animals had missed their targets, his specially trained soldiers would then run underneath the poor beasts and slit their stomachs open.

But there was something even simpler, something that every elephant, according to ancient writers, seemed to fear – the anti-tank weapon of the ancient world: the pig. Elephants can be nervous creatures, which can perhaps be explained by what the Romans did to them in battle, and three authors tell us that the squealing of pigs is what really spooked them. According to the Roman historian Aelian – writing in the late second and early third centuries AD in his book *On the Characteristics of Animals* – when the Romans first came across elephants during Pyrrhus' attack in 280 BC, they quickly worked out that a squealing pig would put the monsters to flight.

Pliny also records this fact, as does the much later Procopius who writes in his book *The Gothic War* that the defenders of cities only had to thrust a squealing pig in the face of an attacking elephant for it to turn on its heels and run.

However, just as it was difficult to make an elephant attack in the first place, it was also not easy to ensure your pigs squealed with enough vigour to put them off. The horrific solution was discovered by the Greeks. When Antigonus II, known as 'Knock-knees' (Gonatas), besieged the city of Megara with elephants, the inhabitants decided to send out squealing pigs. To make certain that the pigs would squeal when some distance away, they first covered them in tar and olive oil and then set fire to them. This certainly had the desired effect of unnerving their enemies, although controlling burning pigs must have proved tricky.

What gave Napoleon's troops sore throats?

The French surgeon D.J. Larrey, First Surgeon of the Imperial Guard, accompanied Napoleon's army during his Egyptian and Middle Eastern campaigns. In his meticulous record of events, one entry rather gruesomely demonstrates that a soldier in an unfamiliar land has far more than just the enemy to worry about.

Larrey describes meeting a soldier of the 69th demi-brigade who had just returned from Syria to the Egyptian fort of Salehyeh. He was complaining of a pricking sensation in his throat and had started to cough up blood. The surgeon proceeded to examine him. 'I interrogated him, and endeavoured, in every way, to discover the cause of these symptoms. By depressing the tongue with a spoon, I discovered the tail of a leech . . . it was about the size of my little finger.'

It turned out that while crossing the scorching desert of Sinai on their return to Egypt, the men had exhausted their water bottles and had taken to drinking from whatever pools could be found at oases. These pools were infested with leeches, which, if the water wasn't strained first, would attach themselves to the soldiers' throats or noses, some even making it down to their stomachs. Larrey notes, with a splendid talent for understatement, that this was 'very inconvenient to the soldiers'. Within days twenty men were complaining of a variety of strange symptoms, from vomiting blood and nosebleeds to shortness of breath (as the leeches swelled with blood and closed off their airways). When they finally arrived back in Egypt, they were all in a serious condition and the surgeon was ordered to do battle with the tenacious creatures. Those deep in the oesophagus were removed by swallowing vinegar, whilst others attached to the throat or the back of the nose were attacked with salt-water gargling and smoking – the unhealthy tobacco fumes apparently encouraging the leeches to unfasten their hold and wriggle out.

In some cases, however, the creature remained doggedly in place and Larrey was reduced to playing a game of cat-and-mouse:

> I immediately introduced a pair of forceps for the purpose of seizing it; but on the first touch it retracted itself behind the velum palati. It became necessary to wait a favourable opportunity to discover it, and when this occurred, with a pair of curved

> polypus forceps, I extracted the reptile at the first attempt. This was attended by a slight haemorrhage, which soon ceased, and in a few days the patient recovered.

Despite these unpleasant infestations, Larrey reported no fatalities.

What happened to the horses after Waterloo?

Some 10,000 horses were killed at the Battle of Waterloo, while many more received shrapnel and blade injuries that left them unfit for further service. As was the habit of the army at this date, those horses too injured to continue service were sold off at an auction, usually going straight to the knacker's yard. Waterloo was different, however, and the up-swelling of popular support for the men who had defeated Napoleon was matched by an outpouring of support for their heroic mounts.

So when the severely injured horses of the Household Brigade of Cavalry came up for auction, twelve of the most hopeless cases found themselves, not en route to the glue factory, but off to the Hertfordshire estate of Sir Astley Paston Cooper, one of the finest surgeons of his generation. At Gadebridge House in Hemel Hempstead, Cooper set about a programme of removing bullets and metal fragments from the old warhorses until, miraculously, they all made full recoveries and could be released into Gadebridge's park.

According to the reminiscences of Captain Gronow, from then on the animals treated their saviour to a show each morning where they would 'form in line, charge and then retreat and afterwards gallop about, appearing greatly contented with the lot which had befallen them'.

Such discipline and strict adherence to army drill was not restricted to Astley's horses; indeed, other tales from the battlefield itself suggest that the cavalry's horses were so well drilled that the scenes in Gadebridge Park were not flights of fancy.

Corporal John Dickson, who charged with the Scots Greys at Waterloo, noted that his horse Rattler received a terrible injury and he only managed to jump clear just before the animal collapsed. Fearing his mount was dead, he grabbed a stray French horse and continued fighting until a French counter-attack forced his unit to withdraw. As his men pulled back in line abreast, he looked up to see Rattler retreating with them in perfect order. It seems the horses of Waterloo knew their duty as well as the soldiers.

What was the War of the Crabs?

The English Civil War was not confined to British shores, nor indeed to solely British combatants, one of the more unusual actions taking place on the other side of the Atlantic and against an enemy that wasn't even human.

Robert Venables was sent to the Caribbean by Oliver Cromwell in December 1654 to attack Spanish possessions there. It was an ill-timed and poorly organised expedition in which command was shared between Venables, who was to take control of the land campaign, and Admiral William Penn. Both men had to confer with a council of three civilians who had knowledge of the territories. No sooner had the party arrived in Barbados in January 1655 than quarrelling immediately broke out. Cromwell had given the expedition a free hand to attack as and where it saw fit but the ill-discipline of the men, and the lack of proper equipment and provisions, made Venables nervous of assailing the wealthy and well-defended Spanish settlements of the New World. In the end it was decided that the island of Hispaniola, nearly 800 miles to the northwest, would make a suitable target as the Spanish settlers were confined, on royal orders, to the area around San Domingo, leaving most of the rest of the island either uninhabited or under the control of pirates.

From the moment they set out, the project seemed doomed. Terrible weather rotted the food and spoilt the gunpowder, whilst their failure to take with them receptacles for storing water meant they could not even save the torrential rain for drinking. Venables was now also barely on speaking terms with Penn and feared his admiral would maroon him as soon as they reached land. The expedition landed forty miles from San Domingo and began marching through dense forest, only to be twice ambushed by the Spanish who had received plenty of warning of their approach. Finally near the settlement of Haina, the army became convinced that they had been surrounded by the Spanish during the night and Venables ordered Penn to evacuate his force.

But according to Spanish accounts there was no Spanish army in the vicinity that night. The rustling through the forest undergrowth that had so frightened the British was actually the migration of thousands of fiddler crabs. Venables had been defeated by a local army of crustaceans.

As some small consolation Venables' force took instead the ill-defended island of Jamaica on their return, founding the settlement of Port Cagway there, which would, rather ironically for a Commonwealth army officer, go on to become Port Royal, and was known as 'the Sodom of the Indies' thanks to its piratical inhabitants. By this time Admiral Penn had dashed for home, keen to report his version of events first. Venables duly chased after him but both, for their troubles, were received back with disgrace and a term in the Tower of London. The crabs' victory was absolute.

What was Blücher's embarrassing secret?

Gebhard Leberecht von Blücher was a sometimes impetuous but brilliant military man, famous today for his timely arrival with the army of the Lower Rhine at the Battle of Waterloo, which helped turn the tide against Napoleon's forces. But, as in so many fields, the difference between military genius and madness is thin and often poorly defined (see page 175), as Wellington found out in the period following the battle.

Immediately after Waterloo there was much to be determined by Wellington and Blücher and their respective countries. The Prussians wanted Napoleon executed to prevent any future 'comebacks' and hoped the battle might go down in history as 'the Battle of La Belle Alliance'. Great Britain, however, was adamant that Napoleon should live and that the battle should be simply called 'Waterloo'. After extensive debates both these matters were finally decided in Great Britain's favour. The time then came for the Duke of Wellington to bid his grateful farewells to Blücher. It should have been a poignant moment as the two great commanders met for the last time, a chance to recall the highs and lows of combat, the dangers, the decisions taken in the heat of the action and, perhaps, a time for them both to congratulate themselves on their handling of the situation. Instead it turned into a catalogue of surprises, for Wellington at least.

Years later Wellington confided what happened at that meeting to Earl Stanhope. Generalfeldmarschall Blücher, the cool-headed man whose intervention swung the battle, let Wellington into a little secret. He announced that at the age of seventy-two he was pregnant, which was certainly in itself unusual. But if Wellington managed to keep his composure at this announcement, the following one must have shaken him. Blücher now announced that he knew what he was carrying. History doesn't record whether Wellington asked, 'A boy or a girl?' but it does record Blücher's answer – an elephant. But it was neither of these two apparently alarming facts that bothered the old Generalfeldmarschall most, as he told his ally. What really galled him was that he had been made pregnant by a French officer. As he said: '*Imaginez que moi – moi – moi! Un soldat français.*'

In fact Blücher had been ill for much of the campaign although his staff had tried to underplay this. He had come to believe that his servants had been paid by the French to heat the floors underneath him so they would burn his feet. He had therefore taken to holding meetings either seated with his feet hovering off the floor, or hopping from foot to foot. In one bout of delirium he had been found fighting the ghost of an officer he had dismissed. In another he had claimed his head was made of stone and begged for someone to hit it with a hammer.

Now he was pregnant, with an elephant and, worst of all, at the hands of the enemy. Wellington offered what assurances he could but behind the cool façade he must have been shocked at the mental state of the ally who had been so vital in the defeat of Napoleon. Waterloo had perhaps been a closer-run thing than he had thought.

Who was stung in the Battle of the Bees?

As a conflict between the world powers of the day, the First World War involved a number of actions outside the theatre of Western Europe, many of which have since been forgotten, and often with good reason. Perhaps the least glorious episode for the British in these colonial campaigns came with the decision to invade German East Africa, which is today Tanzania.

To say that the British Expeditionary Force 'B' was a shade overconfident would be an understatement. Its soldiers were commanded by an old Indian army officer, Arthur Edward Aitken, who was convinced that his men, despite being largely half-trained Indian volunteers, would make short work of the Germans' local black troops.

Aitken's plan relied on surprise, which was unfortunate since his troops had sailed from India – an event widely reported in the press – and had cruised in broad daylight down the coast of East Africa, somewhat advertising their presence in the neighbourhood. They had also been preceded by HMS *Fox*, which had been sent into the busy German East African port of Tanga to inform the governor that the previous truce in the region was off and that he should immediately hand over the port.

When the *Fox* arrived off Tanga, the governor was said to be away. In his place the local German Commissioner, Herr Auracher, was invited on board to take the message. Keen to stall for time, he asked for an hour's grace to go and consult with his superiors, which the captain of the *Fox* granted. The captain also asked whether the harbour was mined and was assured that it was.

Herr Auracher was no fool, unlike his British counterparts, and he immediately rushed to find the German military commander, Colonel von Lettow-Vorbeck, to tell him of the British dispositions. Needless to say, he did not return to HMS *Fox*. After tiring of waiting for his return, the captain of the *Fox* decided to take Tanga harbour anyway but first he had to send in the *Helmuth* to sweep for mines – not that there were any; that had been another of Herr Auracher's little tricks. Meanwhile von Lettow-Vorbeck's men were already on the train and coming to the defence of the port.

While this farcical scene was being played out, Major General Aitken was preparing to land his men two miles upstream at Manza Bay – an entirely inappropriate location in a mangrove swamp, recommended by the captain of the *Fox*. So bad did the ground prove here that it took nearly two days for Aitken to disembark 8,000 men, giving his German counterparts plenty of time to arrive in Tanga and scout out their position.

Aitken, astonishingly, did not feel he needed to reconnoitre and immediately set out for Tanga, walking straight into the enfilading fire of von Lettow-Vorbeck's troops who were waiting to ambush them. Chaos erupted. Some British troops cut their way through to Tanga and seized the customs house but were driven out by naval shelling from HMS *Fox*, which had been ordered to fire on German positions without having any idea where these were. The arrival of German reinforcements – who by now had had plenty of warning of the attack – finally pushed the British out of the town again.

As the British fell back, one final humiliation awaited them. The rifle fire had angered not only the Germans but also the local – and very aggressive – African bees. Finding themselves in a battle they hadn't asked for, these bees promptly set about the retreating British force with as much ferocity as the Germans had. Aitken's men decided the moment had come to save themselves and, abandoning their kit, they ran for the river and the safety of their ships. As well as leaving behind enough ammunition and equipment to resupply the German forces fully, Aitken also left 800 of his men dead, 500 wounded and 250 missing. The Germans, despite having been outnumbered by around eight to one, lost only sixty-nine men. Fortunately for the British, von Lettow-Vorbeck proved to be a gentleman soldier of the old school and, under a flag of truce (and over a bottle of brandy), promised Aitken he would care for his injured men.

The disaster in East Africa was initially covered up by the British government but when news eventually made the press it became clear that a scapegoat would be required. This would not be Major General Aitken, however, or the captain of HMS *Fox*. Even Paul von Lettow-Vorbeck – who remained undefeated for the whole war – wasn't given the satisfaction of being blamed for causing the debacle. Instead the surviving soldiers and the press agreed: the reason the British had been beaten was the Germans' thoroughly unsporting and deliberate use of bees on the battlefield.

Sticks and Stones

An injury is much sooner forgotten than an insult.

Philip Dormer Stanhope, Earl of Chesterfield, *Letters to his Son* (1774), 9 October 1746

How did 'Fighting' Joe Hooker get his name?

Great military leaders often gain colourful epithets designed to flatter them and inspire fear in the hearts of their enemies. Attila was known as 'the scourge of God', which certainly seemed to do the trick. So you might expect to tremble at the sight of the American Civil War general, 'Fighting Joe' Hooker. That is unless you knew how he came by the name.

Joe Hooker was a career soldier for whom the outbreak of the American Civil War offered the perfect getaway from an enforced period as a civilian, following an unfortunate incident in which he had testified against his commanding officer in a court martial. Hooker was ambitious and considered by some of his more staid contemporaries to be rather lively. He greatly enjoyed drinking and gambling, once borrowing money from the legendary General William T. Sherman (which he allegedly never repaid). He was also popular with ladies of 'easy virtue' – or, rather, they were popular with him.

Initially the war favoured Hooker, who was always the first to elaborate his own role in an action and denigrate the incompetence, as he saw it, of his superiors. This seemed to many to be somewhat at odds with the way he led his own life, his command posts being compared to a cross between a brothel and a bar. But Joe Hooker was certainly keen for action. In the US Peninsular campaign he became well known for his aggressive attitude and his open scorn for the over-cautious approach of the commander of the Army of the Potomac, Major General George B. McClellan. His belligerence was particularly approved by the Union press, which felt in need of a good battling leader and it was thanks to them that he got his epithet, although not perhaps in the way he would have wanted.

Writing dispatches for the New York newspaper, *Courier and Enquirer*, on the progress of the peninsular campaign, a reporter penned the headline 'Fighting – Joe Hooker', as a reminder to do a piece about the action in which Joe Hooker had recently been involved. When the article was printed, however, the dash in the headline was omitted and so the legend of 'Fighting Joe Hooker' was born.

Hooker himself is said to have hated the name, claiming it had caused him 'incalculable injury' by suggesting that he was 'a hot-headed, furious young fellow, accustomed to making furious and needless dashes at the enemy'. For many of his commanding officers, that description seemed particularly apt.

The war did not end as well for 'Fighting Joe' as it had begun. Having managed to get General Burnside removed from office, he took command of the Army of the Potomac, only to suffer a comprehensive defeat against General Robert E. Lee's much smaller army at Chancellorsville, despite his pre-battle announcement: 'My plans are perfect and when I start to carry them out, may God have mercy on General Lee, for I will have none.' In response, Lee took to referring to his opponent as 'Mr F.J. Hooker'. Despite these jibes and reverses, he survived the war and died in 1879.

How did a ventriloquist save a soldier's stew?

A good soldier can call on many skills to help him in wartime but few have been more unusual than that of Josias 'Josh' Hetherington. We know of his particular talent thanks to his friend, rifleman Edward 'Ned' Costello, of the 95th Rifles, who wrote an account of their adventures together in the Peninsular War.

Ned Costello evidently found his friend a fascinating man:

> This fellow was one of the queerest I ever met with, and I verily believe had seen service before, but amongst gypsies, prigs [tinkers], gaolbirds, and travelling showmen. There was not a move but what he was up to, and in addition to these, he was an excellent ventriloquist, and terrified the inhabitants as we went along, whenever the occasion offered.

And the occasion did rather fortuitously offer itself.

While the two men were billeted in a house in Portugal they began to notice that their rations and cooking utensils were being tampered with. Secreting themselves in a pantry, they watched as the lady of the house came into the kitchen and tried to steal their meat ration. At this point Josh Hetherington decided to use his ventriloquist skills. As the lady lifted the lid on the pot, he projected his voice with the words, 'Sperum poco' – 'Wait a little.' The lady, believing the words came from the pot, was a little bemused and crossed herself but, overwhelmed by the desire to get her hands on some fresh meat, returned to the business at hand and opened the lid again. Again the words 'Sperum poco' appeared to emanate from the pot. This proved all too much for her. As Ned Costello puts it, this 'sent her reeling and screeching to the corner of the kitchen. "Oh Santa Maria! Oh Jesu, oh la deos! Pedro aye el demonio ei in panello."' Ned helpfully translates; the woman was now convinced that the devil was in the pot and he adds that she made a hasty exit from the kitchen, not returning until Ned, Josh and their possessed pot had moved on.

What did Wellington say behind the marshals' backs?

One of the more socially uncomfortable aspects of war is the chance of coming across old and embittered enemies after hostilities have ceased. Nowhere was this more apparent than in the strange, formal world of the early nineteenth century where men who faced each other across a battlefield one day might face their opponents again across a ballroom the next.

Just such an incident was widely reported at the time to have happened to the Duke of Wellington, following his defeat of Napoleon at Waterloo. Sources vary as to the exact location – some placing it at a ball in his honour in Paris in the spring of 1814, and others at a reception during the Congress of Vienna in the autumn of that year – but everyone agrees on the chain of events.

At this party Wellington swept into the room to find arrayed before him the marshals of France – the very men whom, one by one, Napoleon had thrown against him in the Peninsular War, only for them to be thrown back defeated by the Englishman. For Victor, Jourdan, Marmont, Masséna, Soult and Ney, it had been a humiliation, often the first setback in what had been until that point glittering military careers.

It is therefore not to be wondered at that the Iron Duke was not someone whom they were especially looking forward to meeting again but, even so, it seems that in the heat of the moment their emotions got the better of them. As the duke entered, they sulkily turned their backs on him. The newly installed French Bourbon king Louis XVIII was horrified at this overt insult and rushed to Wellington's side to apologise. Wellington, with his usual sang-froid, dismissed the insult and, as he walked past the marshals, loudly commented: ''Tis of no matter, your Highness, I have seen their backs before!'

How did books save lives in Lucknow?

You really can't beat a good book, as those caught up in the siege of Lucknow during the Indian Mutiny of 1857 could happily testify.

On 30 May that year Lucknow broke out into open rebellion against the British and the city soon became a mustering point for those disaffected by foreign rule. With the rebels gathering outside the city, British citizens, both military and civilian, made for the Residency, a sprawling sixty-acre site that soon contained a garrison of 855 British soldiers, 712 Indian and 153 civilian volunteers, along with 1,280 non-combatants. On 30 June this site began to be bombarded by the rebels, who fired shells at the buildings as well as taking pot-shots with rifles.

The problem for those trapped in the Residency, which was made up of numerous ordinary buildings, was that it wasn't really designed for withstanding a siege. One contemporary account gives an idea of the dangers of living inside:

> On the 22nd of July we experienced another sad casualty in my garrison. Mrs Dorin, one of the Seetapoor refugees, occupied a room on the north side of the upper story [sic] of the house. During the day she was killed by a matchlock ball, which, entering by a window on the south, had traversed two suites of apartments before it reached that in which she was standing.

Clearly some form of makeshift defence was needed and the answer came from the Residency's extensive library. The besieged discovered that by blocking the doorways and windows with bookcases, and then filling them with thick books, they became effectively bulletproof. It was soon being carefully noted which tomes did the best job of stopping enemy fire and which needed to be replaced. In his account of the siege, the Financial Commissioner, Martin Gubbins, observed:

> A volume of Lardner's Encyclopedia receiving a musket-ball on the edge, stopped it after it had penetrated less than halfway through the volume, damaging from a hundred to a hundred and twenty pages. On the other hand, I have seen a quarto volume of Finden's Illustrations of Byron, similarly struck by a three pound ball, and completely destroyed, every page being hopelessly torn and crumpled. It had done its duty, however, for the shot only retained momentum sufficient to force the crumpled mass out upon the floor, and then fell, itself, expended.

Elsewhere even greater libraries were being recruited to play their part in the battle. In L.E. Ruutz Rees' *A Personal Narrative of the Siege of Lucknow*, he stated:

> The splendid library of Captain Hayes, consisting of priceless Oriental manuscripts, and the standard literary and scientific works of every nation of Europe, and dictionaries of every language spoken on earth, from the patois of Bretagne down to

> Cingalese, Malay, and ancient Egyptian, were for the nonce converted into barricades.

Although being almost completely destroyed in the process, the books did their duty and Lucknow was finally evacuated on 19 November. Since first coming under attack, the occupants of the Residency had been besieged and relieved twice, suffering first eighty-seven and then a further sixty-one days under fire. On the most bitter day of fighting, 16 November, twenty-four Victoria Crosses were awarded. Casualty numbers remain uncertain and no one knows how many of the besieged were saved by a good book.

Who was Lady Haw-Haw?

Wartime propaganda can be a two-edged sword, as the pro-German US broadcaster Jane Anderson found to her cost. Just how she ended up broadcasting for the Third Reich is in itself an extraordinary story.

Jane, known as 'the Georgia Peach' to the Americans and 'Lady Haw-Haw' to the English, was born in Atlanta, Georgia, in 1888 and began her professional life as a short-story writer in New York. Having been offered a job as a journalist in England, she became one of the few female reporters to write from the battle front in the First World War. Her reports made her something of a celebrity and she became friends – some sources suggest more than friends – with both H.G. Wells and Joseph Conrad, before eventually marrying a Spanish nobleman, the Marquis Alvarez de Cienfuegos.

The outbreak of the Spanish Civil War meant their happiness was short-lived, however, and her experiences in this conflict, in which she was imprisoned, tortured and sentenced to death by the Loyalists, helped turn her politics towards the heavily anti-communist policies of Nazi Germany. Having been saved from the firing squad by the intervention of the USA, she emerged from the war as a fervent supporter of Franco, earning herself a place in his Ministry of Propaganda. Here she was noticed by the German Reichrundfunk (Empire radio), which offered her a job broadcasting anti-Stalin messages to American troops using the powerful Zeesen transmitter. On 14 April 1941 she made her first broadcast for the Nazis, specialising in interviews that bolstered the Third Reich's anti-communist credentials, including one with William Joyce – the Nazi propagandist known to the British as 'Lord Haw-Haw'. Thereafter she was christened 'Lady Haw-Haw'. She also lavished praise on Hitler, calling him 'an immortal crusader, a great lover of God'.

Her broadcasting career in Germany was brief. Her methods were highly eccentric and she ended each broadcast with the rather peculiar message: 'Always remember progressive Americans eat Kellogg Corn Flakes and listen to both sides of the story.' It was an attempt to boast of how little the war was affecting Berlin that proved her downfall. On 6 March 1942 she reported how she and a friend had visited a Berlin tea shop and enjoyed Turkish cakes, champagne and cognac. This gloating message was designed to demonstrate how the privations of war being suffered by the Allies had barely touched Germany, where everything was still plentiful. It backfired terribly.

The Americans saw an opportunity to use this message against Germany itself. They recorded the broadcast and then played it back to their enemy, where thousands of people heard their own propagandist apparently boasting about the privileged life of cake and champagne being enjoyed by those close to High Command, whilst most Germans were suffering desperate food shortages. The result was outrage among ordinary people. Jane Anderson never made another broadcast and was never heard from again.

How was an earl saved by a beating?

The Battle of Poitiers in 1356 was the second great English victory in the Hundred Years War against France, which would culminate in Henry V's triumph at Agincourt. The Black Prince's tactic of concealing a mobile force in a nearby wood brilliantly outflanked the French, cutting off a party that included the French king John II, leading to his capture and the end of the battle.

King John II was not the only high-value prisoner taken that day. In the aftermath of battle one of the Scottish contingent, Archibald the Grim, Earl of Douglas, was singled out for his fine armour and horse harness, and brought forward. Having been recognised as a valuable prisoner, he was likely to be ransomed back to his family, as indeed the king was for the staggering sum of twice the country's annual income. But, like the king, if he couldn't raise the sum asked, he might simply die in captivity or even be executed.

So, with these unpleasant options before him, Archibald the Grim waited to hear his fate. Fortune smiled on him that day, for among the Englishmen holding him he saw a friendly face, that of Sir William Ramsay of Colluthy. Despite fighting for the English, Ramsay was a kinsman of Douglas's and he determined to get him off the hook.

Not that Douglas can initially have known this. As soon as he appeared, Ramsay launched an elaborate and vitriolic attack on him, calling him a 'damnable murderer' and demanding that he kneel down and remove his boots for him. Removing other people's boots was not something Scottish earls were used to but Douglas had little choice. To add injury to insult, when one boot was off, Sit William seized it and began beating Douglas senseless with it, until others in the party intervened.

Now Sir William's plan finally became clear. When his compatriots told him to stop as he was assaulting someone who was obviously a great lord, he replied that this man was nothing of the sort. Instead he claimed that the man in Douglas's armour was not his cousin but a servant who must have murdered his master and stolen his armour. He then ransomed the supposed servant for forty shillings and ordered him out onto the battlefield again to find the body of the real Douglas and bring it back to him for burial. Adding another few blows around the head for good measure, Sir William then dismissed Douglas who, of course, quickly made his getaway.

What was Pitt's caveat?

In July 1803 there was panic on the south coast of England. Invasion seemed imminent and over that summer some 300,000 men would be enrolled in volunteer corps to defend the nation. Amongst those energetically recruiting men was William Pitt, then Lord Warden of the Cinque Ports. As his biographer Earl Stanhope put it:

> By great activity and energy he had very soon on foot an excellent regiment of Volunteers, divided into three battalions, and numbering three thousand men. He was constantly seen on horseback, and in full Volunteer uniform as the Colonel in chief, exercising and reviewing his men. It was acknowledged on all hands, that as, from the circumstances of the coast, Pitt held the post of principal danger, so he set the most conspicuous example of zeal for the national defence.

But raising volunteer corps was not an easy matter. Being volunteers, these battalions were allowed to draw up their own rules of engagement, which stipulated that they would be used only in the current emergency and not as a cheap army for other government adventures. It was hence Pitt's role to read and approve these terms to ensure his fighting men would and could actually fight. Usually these 'rules' were quite practical and it was simply a matter of form to sign them off, but one battalion's regulations caught his attention.

They appeared to have been drafted by a barrack-room lawyer and were filled with caveats concerning how and when this particular battalion would deign to engage the enemy. Indeed, they were more of a list of what these volunteers wouldn't do rather than what they would, each refusal ending with the proviso 'except in case of invasion'. The last line finished with the simple statement that the unit would never be sent out of the country – to which the exasperated Pitt added the words, 'Except in case of invasion'.

Who was history's first propagandist?

Knowing exactly what happened in wars fought deep in antiquity can be a tricky business. There were often few impartial observers around to write accounts, and the victors tended to embroider their victories with claims of divine interventions and superhuman feats. But thanks to the gargantuan self-publicity machine of Pharaoh Rameses II, and his invention of war reporting, we can glimpse one battle, albeit seen from only one side, that took place in 1274 BC.

The reign of Rameses II saw Egypt develop her empire to its largest extent, reaching from Nubia in the south to Syria in the north. This expansion brought her into conflict with the Middle Eastern Hittite empire. As the two powers vied for influence in the region, war became inevitable and in the fifth year of his reign Rameses set off north to teach the upstart Hittites a lesson.

What is unusual about this campaign is that Rameses clearly decided to have it recorded in detail as it unfolded and the results, obviously massaged somewhat to flatter the pharaoh's ego, were 'published' in two documents known as 'the poem' and 'the bulletin', the first real war reports in history. Despite obviously showing Rameses as the undoubted winner, they also – unusually – mention how he was tricked by his enemy and nearly lost.

While a portion of Rameses' army was camped near Kadesh in what is today Syria, two enemy soldiers who claimed to be deserters were ushered into his presence. When Rameses asked them how near the Hittite army was, their answer was reassuring. The 'bulletin' tells us: 'They said to his Majesty: ". . . the Foe from Hatti is in the land of Khaleb to the north of Tunip. He was too fearful of Pharaoh to come southward when he heard that Pharaoh had come northward."'

Rameses could relax. The huge Hittite army was still 120 miles to the north. There was plenty of time for the rest of the Egyptian army to catch up with him. Then, two more enemy soldiers were dragged into Rameses' royal tent and questioned. Given that the Hittite army was supposedly over 100 miles away, why were Hittite scouts snooping around Kadesh? Rameses' suspicions were confirmed by their response: 'Look, the Vile Chief of Hatti has come together with the many countries that are with him . . . They are more numerous than the sands of the shore. Look, they stand equipped and ready to fight behind Kadesh the Old.'

This came as a bit of a shock to Rameses. The massive Hittite army was not 120 miles to the north, but just over the next hill. Worse still, most of his own army had not yet reached him in the camp. Frantically, Rameses sent orders for his divisions to move up to his position as quickly as possible. It was too late. Before the rest of the Egyptian troops had arrived, the Hittite army attacked.

The situation was critical. The pharaoh of Egypt stood on the brink of defeat. As they had given such an honest account this far, it is perhaps not surprising that the record here becomes a little more florid. Rameses now spins a tale that turns defeat into victory and transforms him from a gullible commander into a godlike warrior.

> When his majesty caught sight of [the enemy] he rose quickly . . . Taking up weapons and donning his armour . . . he mounted 'Victory-in-Thebes', his great horse, and started out quickly alone by himself . . .
>
> All his ground was ablaze with fire, he burned all the countries with his blast. His eyes were savage as he beheld them; his power flared like fire against them. He heeded not the foreign multitude; he regarded them as chaff.

Charge!

As his records tell it, Rameses charged the entire Hittite army single-handed, while his men fled around him, ignoring his rallying cries. Even without the help of his troops, he still claims to have routed the enemy:

> there was no high officer with me, no charioteer, no soldier, no shield bearer, my infantry and chariotry scampering away before them . . . Not one of them stood firm to fight with me . . .
>
> My majesty caused the forces of the foes from Hatti to fall on their faces . . . I was after them like a griffin . . . As I live . . . everything that my majesty has told I did it in truth.

One should always be wary of narratives that end with 'and that's the truth – honest' and this is no exception. What actually must have happened is that the Egyptian relief column arrived in time and drove the Hittites back.

Back home, the war reports became part of the first great propaganda campaign in history. Rameses had the victory at Kadesh carved onto just about every spare piece of temple he could find, always with himself charging into the enemy single-handed in his chariot. But behind the scene there was some Realpolitik going on. Whilst the pharaoh still described his enemy as the 'vile chief of Hatti' in official inscriptions, in his diplomatic correspondence with the Hittites he now refers to him as 'Great King and brother'.

Which monument tells both sides of the story?

The story of Napoleon's fateful attack on Russia in 1812 has been told many times, both to emphasise the hubris of the great French general in believing he could take on such a vast nation and its cruel winter weather, and to demonstrate the extraordinary sacrifices that the Russians were prepared to make to save their country.

Indeed, in the summer of 1812 as Napoleon's army headed east, few believed it could ever be stopped. The news that the

Grande Armée was routed and in full retreat was initially met with disbelief, even by Napoleon's enemies, who took the news that Moscow was in flames to mean that the French had taken the city. In fact the Russians had set their city alight themselves to deny Napoleon the shelter and provisions he needed if his army was to survive the winter.

Napoleon was forced into a disastous withdrawal where hunger, frostbite and disease proved as deadly as the Russians who harried his retreat. When Napoleon had passed through the city in the summer of 1812, he had commented that it was 'the Jerusalem of the north'. So enchanted had he been by the tiny church of St Ann that he had said that on his return he would like to pick it up in his hand and carry it away to Paris. Just a few months later Robert Wilson, a British officer attached to the Russian General Staff, gave this very different view of the French hospital now set up in the city:

> The hospital presented the most awful and hideous sight: 7,500 bodies were piled up like pigs of lead [lead ingots] over one another in the corridors. Carcasses were strewed about in every part; and all the broken windows and walls were stuffed with feet, legs, arms, hands, trunks and heads to fit the apertures, and keep out the air from the yet living.

But the story was told at its most simple and devastating on a monument in the city. On the side facing Moscow was inscribed: 'Napoleon Bonaparte passed this way in 1812 with 400,000 men.' On the opposite side were the words: 'Napoleon Bonaparte passed this way in 1812 with 9,000 men.'

In the Unlikely Event . . .

Always mystify, mislead, and surprise the enemy, if possible.

Thomas Jonathan 'Stonewall' Jackson, quoted in M. Miner and H. Rawson, *American Heritage Dictionary of American Quotations* (1997)

How did a wrong turn start a war?

The First World War was begun, as every schoolchild knows, by the assassination of the Archduke Franz Ferdinand, heir to the Austro-Hungarian empire, by a member of a group of Serbian separatists. The exact reasons why such an occurence led to such a war is a matter for a much weightier book than this but what is interesting is that the assassination happened, and hence the First World War perhaps started, only because of a wrong turning.

The organiser of the assassination attempt, Danilo Ilic, was thorough and had recruited four men to each have a go at killing the archduke as he drove through the streets of Sarajevo on 28 June 1914, arming them with pistols, bombs, grenades and cyanide capsules (to prevent their being captured alive). Things had not gone to plan, however, and as Franz Ferdinand's open-topped Gräf & Stift car passed by the first would-be assassin, Mehmed Mehmedbasic, he froze and failed to throw his bomb. So did Vaso Cubrilovic, who was standing next to him. Further down the route, Nedeljko Cabrinovic proved himself made of sterner stuff and he did throw his bomb, but it bounced off the folded cover of the archduke's car and exploded under the car behind, wounding twenty people. Cabrinovic, unwilling to be captured, now swallowed his cyanide pill and jumped into the Miljacka river for good measure. Sadly for him, the pill proved ineffective and the Miljacka was only four inches deep. Having been neither poisoned nor drowned, he was instead hauled off by the police.

The archduke was now understandably flustered but he went on with the day's events, attending a reception in the town hall. After this he and his wife decided to abandon their original plan and go and visit the hospital treating those injured in the earlier attack. At this same time the fourth potential assassin, Gavrilo Princip, had just found out that Cabrinovic's assassination attempt had failed and he was consoling himself with a sandwich from Schiller's delicatessen. As he emerged from the shop, he had a shock. There in front of him was the archduke's open-topped car slowly reversing, with the archduke and his wife sitting in the back. No one had told its driver, Franz Urban, about the plan to visit the hospital and he had continued on the original route out of town until being told to double back. As he attempted this manoeuvre, Princip seized the day. Dashing forward, he pulled out his semi-automatic pistol and fired two shots, fatally injuring the archduke and his wife.

Franz Ferdinand's last words, to his wife, were reported as, 'Soferl, Soferl! Don't die. Live for our children!' She was unable to comply and died fifteen minutes later, followed moments afterwards by her husband. Thus the stage was set for the First World War.

What war started when the fat lady sang?

The revolutionary war that brought the nation of Belgium into being was inspired, astonishingly, by a rather stirring aria in an opera about a girl who ends up throwing herself into Mount Vesuvius.

Following the defeat of Napoleon, the Congress of Vienna in 1814–15 had created a kingdom for the House of Orange-Nassau, made up of what is today the Netherlands and Belgium, and grandly called 'The United Kingdom of the Netherlands'. Whilst it is easy to create nations on paper, it can be a lot harder to live in them and the Walloons of the Belgian part of the new state were particularly annoyed by the situation. They were Catholic, unlike their new monarch William I, and it was clear from the start that the king and his ministers would put the Dutch Protestant part of their country first and foremost in all things.

By 1830 the political temperature was rising; in July of that year the revolution took place in neighbouring France, and the Belgians eagerly followed suit. What fanned the spark of discontent into the flames of revolution was a song. On the night of 25 August 1830 there was a performance at the Théâtre de la Monnaie in Brussels of what is probably the earliest French grand opera – *La Muette de Portici* (*The Mute Girl of Portici*) by Daniel Auber, in honour of the birthday of the widely disliked William I. The key aria in the opera was the duet 'Amour sacré de la patrie' ('Sacred love of the motherland'), a rousing piece that so inflamed the Belgian audience that they streamed from the theatre shouting patriotic slogans. No one had really expected a night at the theatre to have quite this effect and thus the Dutch authorities were taken completely by surprise when opera-goers started seizing government buildings.

Riots spread until on 1 September the Estates-General managed to convince the Crown Prince William, later William II, that the only solution was to separate the north and south administratively. The king refused and sent in the army, which despite fierce engagements failed to take Brussels. In late September, a provisional government was declared in the city and on 4 October a declaration of independence was made. King William, still reluctant to lose a part of his nice new country, continued fighting and refused to accept the inevitable until 1835, when the Treaty of London forced him to admit that Belgium now well and truly existed.

How did the French get to the trenches?

By the end of August 1914, Germany's plans for a quick and decisive war in Europe seemed on the verge of being realised. Following the Schlieffen plan, the German army had swept through neutral Belgium and the three armies on her right wing were closing in on Paris. With the British Expeditionary Force and the French 5th and 6th armies in retreat, the situation looked desperate. The French government abandoned the capital and moved to Bordeaux, and by the first week of September nearly half a million Parisians had evacuated their city. So confident indeed was the German commander, General von Kluck, that it was said he had already booked rooms for himself and his General Staff at the Paris Ritz.

With few options remaining, the French commander, General Joffre, decided the best form of defence was attack and on 6 September he threw 150,000 men against the flank of the German 1st army in what became known as the First Battle of the Marne. Surprised by this counter-attack, von Kluck wheeled his entire army around to face the French, in the process opening up a fifty-kilometre-wide gap between his army and that of General von Bülow. Seizing this opportunity, the British Expeditionary Force and the 5th army forced their way into the gap, dividing the German forces and bringing their advance to a halt.

For three days the Germans tried to break through and reconnect. Being attacked on two sides and suffering heavy casualties, the French found themselves on the brink of collapse. What they desperately needed were reinforcements for their exhausted men but there seemed no way to get them to the battlefield in time.

It was at this point that a rather unusual vehicle drew up, filled with fresh French troops – a Parisian taxi. And it was not the only one. Indeed, there was a convoy of some 600, stretching over three kilometres. The military governor in Paris, hearing of the desperate situation, had commandeered all the taxis in the city and filled them with 6,000 reserve troops who now arrived ready for battle. With these reinforcements, the French line held and the German armies were kept apart. On 9 September, the German commander-in-chief, General von Moltke, announced that he had had enough; von Kluck and von Bülow's armies were ordered to withdraw and regroup on the Aisne river. The German plans for a quick victory had been stalled and Paris was saved, thanks to her taxis. The mobile war was over and the era of trench warfare about to begin.

What was a Waterloo smile?

Throughout the history of warfare the morning after battle finds scavengers, both animal and human, working their way through the dead and dying, looking for anything that might prove profitable. But the valuables on a fallen soldier didn't necessarily end with his rings, watch and personal effects. They might include parts of his body as well.

During the eighteenth century improvements in dental surgery had allowed the creation of reasonably good denture plates made of ox bone or hippo ivory – something of a necessity among the upper classes of Europe whose sweet tooth often left their own teeth unfit for purpose. The problem for dentists, however, was getting good-quality teeth to put in dentures, particularly front teeth, which were the most 'on show'. Teeth receive a lot of punishment and are subject to huge pressures so a very hard material is needed. Some dentists favoured carving teeth from elephant or walrus ivory but bone and ivory, lacking a hard enamel casing, quickly decayed, leaving the wearer with pitted teeth and foul-smelling breath. Easily the best answer for most seemed to be human teeth. The problem with human teeth, of course, was that most people with a decent set were using them and were quite naturally loath to part with them. There was a lucrative trade in the teeth of executed criminals, especially young ones, but not everyone wanted such ghoulish trophies. Furthermore, at over £30 (over £3,000 today) for a genuine human upper row – a London price in the 1780s – few could afford the real thing.

There was one source, however and, after 18 June 1815, supply suddenly increased. Tens of thousands of young, fit men died in the Battle of Waterloo and the trade in their healthy, strong teeth soon boomed. Teeth were removed from the fallen of both sides and shipped by the barrel load to England as the 'teeth of heroes', which the more fashionable and toothless elements of society soon began to flaunt with some pride. Needless to say, some dandies sporting a heroic Waterloo smile were actually wearing the teeth of Prussians or even dead enemy Frenchmen, but the exact origin of each set doesn't seem to have bothered the wearers and flashing the teeth of brave Englishmen actually became something of a patriotic statement. No one seems to have asked the relatives of these unwitting teeth donors what they thought of the opportunists scouring the battlefield and burial sites, pliers in hand, looking to make a quick profit.

The craze for soldiers' teeth continued up to the 1840s when porcelain alternatives, and changing sensibilities, put an end to the trade. Even into the 1860s, however, those in Europe who preferred 'real' dentures could buy the teeth of soldiers who had fallen in the American Civil War, which were shipped over for discerning clients.

How did an Orange cure scurvy?

In August 1624, the Dutch fortress city of Breda was encircled by a Spanish army led by Ambrosio Spinola. Conditions in the city during the ensuing eleven-month siege were horrific, as might be expected. The States of Holland had taken some care to prepare the city and had laid in supplies of rye, cheese and dried fish, but the rye had been in storage for thirty years and was, in all honesty, somewhat past its best. The cheese was also rotten and of little nutritional value. So the inhabitants turned to eating dog and horseflesh to supplement their meagre, mouldy diet.

What happened next remains hard to explain. The autumn of 1624 was wet and unhealthy, the diet of the besieged was abysmal and hence outbreaks of disease and malnutrition were to be expected. So when the doctors announced an outbreak of scurvy this was hardly surprising. The strange thing was that this appeared to be an outbreak of *infectious* scurvy, something we now know to be impossible as the disease is a result of vitamin C deficiency, hence not contagious.

Soon hundreds of people were reporting symptoms including livid spots on their skin, loss of teeth, wasting and paralysis. The doctors insisted that the disease was clearly scurvy, although this can be very difficult to diagnose, but claimed that it was exacerbated – and, indeed, made infectious – by grief and disappointment. And in that rather odd statement lay a clue to the cure.

By 20 March 1625, 1,608 soldiers in the garrison were reporting symptoms and the doctors had despaired of a remedy. On 2 May the news of the imminent collapse of the garrison from disease reached the Prince of Orange, accompanied by the information that the disease was encouraged and possibly caused by 'grief'. The prince's response was as unusual as it was successful.

Along with letters promising a speedy relief, he sent a batch of small vials of 'medicine', which he claimed was immensely powerful and would cure the sickness. Three of these were given to each doctor in the city, together with instructions that the tincture was so strong that just three or four drops could be added to a gallon of liquor and that would suffice. Although the homeopathic remedy he sent was at the time believed to be effective, the usual dose was a vial and a half per person. The Prince of Orange had nowhere near that amount, hence the deception.

The results were amazing, as the Dutch physician Frederick van der Mye recorded:

> We now displayed our wonder-working balsams. Nor were even the commanders let into the secret of the cheat put upon the soldiers. They flocked in crowds about us, every one soliciting that part may be reserved for their use. Cheerfulness again appears on every countenance; and universal faith prevails in the sovereign virtues of the remedy.

To give the medicine an extra 'kick' and thus encourage the taker to believe in its efficacy, the doctors began adding camphor and wormwood to the concoction to make it taste stronger. And, sure enough, they did believe: 'The effect however of the delusion was really astonishing: for many were quickly and perfectly recovered. Such as had not moved their limbs for a month before, were seen walking the streets sound, upright, and in perfect health. They boasted of their cure by the Prince's remedy.'

Clearly the psychological effects of the siege were a major factor in the Breda 'disease', which the Prince of Orange, with great forethought, managed to counter using the then unheard of 'placebo effect'. Sadly for Breda, the 'cure' came too late. In June 1625, Justin of Nassau surrendered the city to the Spanish.

What did two lost Germans start by accident?

Although it would be wrong to say that the Blitz on London in the second half of 1940 was a 'mistake', it did very probably start out as a navigational misunderstanding. Following the fall of France on 22 June, the German High Command had hoped that the British would capitulate but, when it became clear that this would never happen, Operation Sealion, the plan to invade Britain, was made ready.

The first stage required that the Luftwaffe achieve at least air superiority, if not air supremacy, over their RAF counterparts and their failed attempts to do this have been known ever since as the 'Battle of Britain'. The next stage, however, had more to do with luck than judgment.

On 8 August 1940, the Luftwaffe was ordered to extend its bombing operations to British industrial targets including ports and harbours, expanding this from 12 August to take in airfields and factories. For many, the threatened invasion now seemed imminent, with the ports being softened up, and the RAF that the Luftwaffe couldn't defeat in the air being bombed into submission on the ground. But towards the end of August, Hitler suddenly, and perhaps fortunately for Britain, changed his bombing policy, all thanks to a navigational error.

On the night of 24 August 1940, a new night-bombing campaign was instigated and that evening ten (some sources say eleven) Heinkel He111 bombers flew over the Channel towards their targets – the port facilities at Thames Haven on the lower Thames. Their targets were still very definitely industrial, not civilian, but during this first night-time raid at least two of the Heinkels got lost. What happened next is a matter of conjecture but, whether in the belief that they were over their real target or in a panicked attempt to get home, the planes discharged their bomb load over London, killing nine civilians and destroying a statue of Milton in Cripplegate.

Winston Churchill was incensed that non-combatants were being targeted and ordered a retaliatory raid on Berlin the following night. Strangely enough, it seems that Hitler was also incensed that this might have handed the British a propaganda victory and no further night-time London raids followed. Indeed, there are suggestions that the pilots concerned were reprimanded.

A further British raid on Berlin, however, killed civilians and a third on the night of 3 September gave Hitler the opportunity to claim that his decision to attack civilian targets now was simply in retaliation for Churchill's own expansion of the scope of the war. Two days later he issued an order 'for disruptive attacks on the population and air defences of major British cities, including London, by day and night'. On 7 September, the Blitz began.

How did horses defeat the Dutch navy?

Losing a battle is hard enough to bear when you are beaten by a greater force of the same type. It is still worse to lose to an inferior force, but to lose to an entirely inappropriate force really is beyond the pale (see pages 118 & 121).

Yet this is what awaited the Dutch navy in 1795. On continental Europe, in the winter of that year, the French revolutionary wars were still raging. In Holland, as elsewhere, it was a dangerous time for the ruling elites as popular sentiment among the people often sided with the French. In particular the ruler, or stadtholder, of the Dutch republic, William V Batavus, Prince of Orange, had reason to fear both the French and his own people. His had been a long minority as he had inherited his throne at the age of three and a series of regents ruling in his name had ushered in an era of staggering corruption. Not surprisingly, he was deeply unpopular but he took some comfort, as have rulers before and since, from the nature of his land.

Holland was (and is) low-lying and criss-crossed with canals and dykes, making it difficult to invade. The young Queen Wilhelmina of the Netherlands would later sum this up very nicely when, during a meeting with the Kaiser before the outbreak of the First World War, he teased her that his guards were seven feet tall and would tower over hers. She famously replied: 'Quite true, Your Majesty, your guards are seven feet tall. But when we open our dykes, the water is ten feet deep!'

What the stadtholder William and, indeed, his army had failed to take into account, however, was the fact that the January of 1795 was the coldest on record. The waterways that might normally have held up an invader were frozen solid. Even the sea around the coast had frozen. The French general, Jean-Charles Pichegru, seized the opportunity to invade. The land war was a rout. The French entered Amsterdam on 18 January to the cheers of the crowd, whilst the last stadtholder slipped out of Holland, never to return. In England, one of the cornerstones of the alliance against France, it was clear that Holland would fall. The British took advantage of the situation by helping themselves to forty Dutch warships, carrying them off to England to prevent them falling into French hands.

And onward the French army swept, across the frozen Lake Biesbos, into the great arsenal at Dordrecht, and through Rotterdam to The Hague. Here Pichegru learnt that the rest of the Dutch fleet, a still sizeable and potentially formidable force, lay off the island of Texel to the north. Normally such a fleet would have been proof against a French land force, but, like the Dutch army, the navy had been caught unprepared by the extreme temperatures and were frozen in. Not expecting to see action until the sea-ice melted, they were not on their guard and therefore not expecting what happened next. Pichegru ordered a detachment of cavalry to make a bold dash across the frozen waters of the Zuyder Zee, whose ice proved so thick that the unit was able to ride right up to the Dutch fleet and surround it. The admiral and captains of the fleet had never been attacked by cavalry before – it was not normally the sort of thing you come across when afloat – and were so startled that they simply surrendered.

How was Sergeant Clifton saved by a turnip?

Just before the Battle of Ramnagar, on 22 November 1848, in the Second Sikh War between British and Sikh forces, Sergeant Clifton of the 14th, the King's Light Dragoons, happened to have a moment to pick some vegetables. An army marches of course on its stomach and Sergeant Clifton's stomach had suggested to him that he should stop in the turnip field that lay before him and help himself.

Such opportunistic foraging was all part of the lot of the British soldier whose food supplies could be variable in both quantity and quality, particularly when in distant parts of the empire such as north-west India. Clifton was about to make the most of his opportunity when, somewhat inconveniently, the bugles sounded for him to prepare for action.

The 14th had been ordered forward towards the Sikh forces occupying the Ramnagar crossing of the Chenab river. Not knowing when another such turnip field might present itself to him, Clifton quickly pulled up a good-sized root and popped it under his shako (a tall cylindrical military cap) for later, before mounting up and heading into battle.

The Battle of Ramnagar was a decidedly bloody affair, in which the Sikh commander, Sher Singh Attariwalla, initially outgunned the British artillery before throwing forward 3,000 of his cavalry. The brunt of this attack was felt by the 14th Dragoons and Sergeant Clifton, who repulsed the attack only to find themselves drawn into the enemy artillery fire. As they reeled from this, the Sikh cavalry turned and attacked again.

Vicious hand-to-hand fighting now ensued, during which Sergeant Clifton's horse was shot from under him. Thrown to the ground, he was surrounded by Sikh swordsmen who repeatedly slashed at his head before he could be rescued by his men.

Eventually the Sikh forces withdrew across the Chenab but only after inflicting heavy losses on the British. Brigadier Cureton, widely recognised as the best cavalry commander in the army, was dead, as was the commanding officer of the 14th Light Dragoons. Sergeant Clifton, despite his ordeal, was fine, however. Once he was safely back behind his own lines, an inspection of his headgear showed that his shako had been cut to ribbons by sword thrusts in the attack but his head remained untouched, thanks to the stoical turnip that he had secreted there, which, though now only suitable for soup, had saved his life.

What was the Old Man's Company?

War is often considered to be a young man's game, particularly the bit that actually involves fighting, but extraordinary causes sometimes call for extraordinary measures. The American Revolutionary War was just the sort of conflict that could bring more unusual combatants into the field, fired with a love of their fledgling country and a desire to see it freed from foreign control. One does wonder, however, whether enthusiasm rather overtook ability in some cases.

Such an incident is recorded in the *Pennsylvania Mercury* newspaper for 9 June 1775. Pennsylvania was already noted for the ardour with which its German and Swiss inhabitants took up the cause of revolution against British rule. Whole towns were swept along on a wave of patriotic fervour, the men marching in recruitment parades at weekends whilst their wives and daughters raised money to fund still more companies.

So it was that by mid-1775 the small town of Reading had already raised three companies, accounting for just about every available man in the area. Such was the popular zeal that no one wanted to be left out and the *Pennsylvania Mercury* noted with some pride the formation of a more unusual fourth company.

The Old Man's Company certainly lived up to its name. It consisted of eighty Germans, all aged forty and upwards, who had previously been considered too old to serve. If the forty-year-olds were old, they were nothing compared to the man who led them into the field, who was ninety-six. If youth was no longer on his side, he could at least claim experience. He had been in the regular army in Germany for forty years and had been involved in seventeen pitched battles. With his sprightly eighty-four-year-old drummer boy at his side, he proposed that his men go into battle, not with the traditional cockade in their hats, but 'a black crepe, as expressive of their sorrow for the mournful events which have occasioned them, at their late time of life, to take arms against our brethren, in order to preserve that liberty which they left their native country to enjoy'.

If the Old Man's Company ever did see action, there is no record of it.

Non-Combatants

The innocent are so few that two of them seldom meet – when they do, their victims lie strewn around.

Elizabeth Bowen, *The Death of the Heart* (1938), pt 1, ch. 8

Why did the Russian fleet attack a trawler?

The story of the Russian Grand Fleet's journey from the Baltic to its ultimate destruction by the Japanese fleet at Tsushima Bay in 1905 is a catalogue of disasters that could fill several books on its own, yet one particular incident stands out for its tragic ineptitude.

That the Russian fleet embarking from the Baltic was poorly prepared, manned by largely untrained crews and provided with often second-rate equipment, is undisputed but, in the face of a war with Japan, Admiral Rozhdestvenski had to make do. What is more inexplicable is his crews' entire lack of geographical understanding and inability to tell friend from foe. It is only thanks to their general incompetence at gunnery that more 'friends' weren't sent to the bottom en route.

This was amply demonstrated, not in the waters off Japan, but off the Dogger Bank in the North Sea. The Russian fleet was nervous of attack from Japanese motor boats although no one seems to have told the crews that the North Sea – on the other side of the world from Japan and dominated by the world's greatest naval power of the day, Britain – was not a usual sphere of operation for such vessels. It was just after midnight on the morning of 22 August, as the Russian fleet steamed through the North Sea, that bugles began to sound and klaxons wailed, announcing that the Russians were under attack. All hell then broke loose as the Russian ships' searchlights scanned the dark seas for enemy vessels and the big guns of the fleet opened up.

On board the Hull-based Gamecock fleet, there was also a degree of panic. They had been quietly fishing the Dogger Bank, as they traditionally did, only minutes earlier, but now they found themselves under attack from an unknown enemy. Joseph Smith on the *Crane* had woken to the noise and, running to the bridge of the little boat, found his father and the third hand both headless in a pool of blood, having taken a direct hit. The first hand was on deck, frantically waving a red lamp at the unseen assailants, whilst three other trawlers heroically braved the hail of fire to come alongside the *Crane* to take off the survivors. Illuminated in the searchlights from the Russian battleships, the crews stood on deck, desperately waving fish to show they were unarmed.

At this point the trawler fleet was saved from annihilation by a further piece of spectacular bungling. The Russian cruiser squadron, which should have been fifty miles away, had seen the firing and decided to return fire – shelling its own battleships – and so a firefight developed between the two elements of the fleet. Seven battleships now pounded two of their own cruisers, the battleship *Oryol* alone loosing off over 500 shells, although fortunately her gunnery was so breathtakingly bad that she recorded not a single hit. Other ships proved little better. The cruiser *Aurora* received just four hits, one of which cut the ship's chaplain in two. Although their ship had not been hit at all, some of the crew of the *Borodino*, obviously fearing the worst, had donned lifejackets and jumped into the sea just in case.

When the mistake was finally realised and the shelling stopped, the fleet steamed off, leaving the Gamecocks to fend for themselves, some of the Russian commanders still, insanely, believing that they had sunk a Japanese task force hiding among the fishermen. Perhaps not surprisingly there was outrage in Britain. A large Royal Navy fleet henceforth shadowed the hapless Russians through the Bay of Biscay and out of range of British trawlers.

Whose Crimean reforms put the British army back on their feet?

Florence Nightingale has gained a reputation as one of the foremost army reformers of her generation, thanks to her tireless efforts to improve conditions for troops at the British army hospital at Scutari, during the Crimean campaign. So bright indeed has the reputation of the 'Lady with the Lamp' burnt that it has all but obscured the story of another great reformer without whom the British army would have been in a truly sorry state.

Alexis Soyer was a French chef who had escaped to Britain after the July revolution of 1830 in France, when his services as chef to Prince Polignac were suddenly no longer required. Having a reputation as a brilliant cook and a great innovator, Soyer rapidly found employment, first with the Duke of Cambridge, before becoming *chef de cuisine* at the newly opened Reform Club in 1837. The kitchens that he and Charles Barry designed together included numerous novelties – cooking on gas, refrigeration, and even thermostats on the cookers. Soyer's mastery of these earned him the impressive salary of nearly £1,000 per annum.

But Alexis Soyer had a conscience that would not let him rest on his laurels. During the Great Potato Famine in Ireland, he became so concerned that nothing was being done to alleviate the situation that he wrote to the press and in April 1847 was appointed by the government to go to Dublin to set up his own invention – the soup kitchen – which sold well-cooked soup and meat at half the usual price. He also took time there to write a sixpenny book, *Soyer's Charitable Cookery*, much of the proceeds of which was given to the poor.

In 1855 it was to another malnourished part of society that Soyer turned when, on 2 February, he wrote to *The Times*, offering to travel, at his own expense, to the Crimea. News was filtering back from the British camps there, largely due to reports in *The Times*, that poor hygiene, inadequate medical care and inept food provision were having as damaging an effect on the British troops as the enemy. The British government were loath to let Soyer go, but, thanks to the powerful connections he had made while cooking for the London elite, he was finally given permission to sail. In the Crimea he discovered an antiquated cooking system that was regularly poisoning its own men. Each soldier received his own ration, which he would usually boil in a communal pot, adding a button or coin to the food so that he could identify his own portion after cooking. The food frequently contained raw and cooked meat mixed together, was prepared on filthy surfaces and was put in dirty containers. Those portions nearer the edge of the cooking pot were often not cooked at all and any one tainted ration soon infected all the others.

Soyer immediately set to work, inventing a portable army field stove, which worked in all conditions and which would heat food through thoroughly. He also began training soldiers as cooks to take charge of food preparation for each regiment. The button-and-coin system was halted and each soldier handed his ration over to a cook, who prepared and distributed meals for the whole regiment together. At Scutari, Soyer also met Florence Nightingale and began revising the dietary sheets for the injured, drastically reducing the incidence of food poisoning and improving their recovery time. Indeed, so impressive were his results that the *Morning Chronicle* announced, 'he saved as many lives through his kitchens as Florence Nightingale did through her ward.'

Soyer returned to England in May 1857 and continued to develop his ideas for army cooking, lecturing at the United Services Institution and building a model kitchen at Wellington barracks. He also produced a book that deftly combined his harrowing experiences in the Crimea with handy recipes, entitled *Soyer's Culinary Campaign*, which, the publishers claimed, 'will carry economy and an improved bill of fare into every household, and prove an inestimable boon to every housekeeper in the kingdom'.

Soyer's role in improving the fighting efficiency of the British army by taking to heart that old French dictum that an army marches on its stomach has had a huge influence on British military thinking. His 'Soyer Stove' became a regular piece of kit, being phased out only in the late twentieth century, and the use of regimental chefs was extended across the army. However, never let it be said that the establishment makes hasty changes – it would be 1945 before the Army Catering Corps that he had envisaged would actually be set up.

Alexis Soyer died on 5 August 1858, his health having been fundamentally undermined by the arduousness of his work in the Crimea. He was buried in Kensal Green cemetery under a memorial to 'Faith'. All his papers were seized by a creditor and have since disappeared, consigning to oblivion a man whose stove was once as important to the war effort as a certain lady's lamp. No official recognition or thanks was ever forthcoming from his adoptive country.

What was Boney's sheepish plan?

There are many contingencies to be considered on the home front in any war where there is a threat of invasion. With the outbreak of the First World War, the British Home Command was forced to consider an eventuality that hadn't been thought likely since the days of Napoleon.

Committees were soon considering plans as diverse as the removal of road signs to baffle the invaders and the possibility of destroying all stocks of beer and spirits in pubs, presumably to prevent the despairing British from simply getting drunk – although it was pointed out that letting the enemy drink the beer might slow them down enough for British forces to regroup.

For one of the young officers, J.F.C. Fuller – known as 'Boney' to his friends, who would go on to become a legend in the General Staff – his pressing concern was sheep. In the opening winter of the war he had been asked to look into a particularly knotty problem – what to do with all the sheep in Sussex, Kent and Surrey in the event of invasion. It was probably not something that was bothering the sheep or even their shepherds, but the Home Command was insistent that this valuable commodity of several million heads of livestock shouldn't fall into enemy hands.

So Fuller was given the job of organising their evacuation. According to the plan, as soon as news reached the General Staff that an invasion was under way, all 5 million or so animals were to be immediately route-marched to Salisbury Plain. Fuller knew this to be an insane idea but orders were orders and so he began drawing up sheep transport timetables. It became obvious from these that the manoeuvre would involve blocking just about every road in southern England for days, a fact that he decided to mention to his superior. The sage-like general, however, taking the whole matter very seriously, simply agreed and said: 'Of course, at once arrange to have a number of signposts ready and marked "Sheep are not to use this road".'

The exasperated Fuller, with perhaps a slightly better knowledge of sheep logistics than his general, simply replied: 'But what if the less well-educated sheep are unable to read them?' This, as he put it, 'brought our conversation to an end'.

Which British soldier gave birth to a daughter?

You can meet all sorts of people on a battlefield but you don't often get to meet someone as particular as Mother Ross. Her exploits at the end of the seventeenth and the beginning of the eighteenth century, immortalised in a work by Daniel Defoe, made her one of the most unlikely military heroes of the age.

Mother Ross started life in Ireland, where her father had lost his fortune fighting at the Battle of the Boyne. Being destitute, she had been sent to live with an aunt in Dublin who ran a pub. On that aunt's death, she had inherited the business and married her waiter, one Thomas Walsh. At this point the settled life of an innkeeper seemed to beckon, were it not for an unfortunate accident.

Thomas Walsh had gone out to pay the brewer's bill when he met an old friend who tempted him aboard a ship for a drink. Many hours and many drinks later, Thomas found himself off the Dutch coast and, with no money to buy a passage home, he decided he had no choice other than to enlist. Twelve months passed before any news reached Dublin of Thomas, in which time his wife and children had given him up for dead. Finally a letter arrived explaining his predicament and Mrs Walsh, whom one biographer refers to as having 'a romping disposition', decided to join up too and go and find him.

Having placed her children with relatives, she disguised herself as a man and enlisted as Christopher Walsh, being shortly after shipped to Holland to fight in the Nine Years War. Here it seems she rather took to the soldier's life and for a while forgot all about searching for her husband. It was reported that she was always in the thick of the fighting, receiving a musket wound at the Battle of Landen and once even being taken prisoner. Off the battlefield she found military pastimes equally to her liking and it was said that she 'romped with every female who gave her the least encouragement'.

Having been discharged from her regiment, after pressure from a local burgher with whose daughter Walsh had had an affair, she immediately re-enlisted in another regiment (Lord Hay's Regiment of Dragoons) and was again wounded, this time at Donawert. Shortly afterwards, much to her surprise, she ran into her husband. He too was a little surprised, not least because he was in the arms of a Dutch woman at the time. However, the two agreed to keep their secret until after the war and so Mrs Walsh was able to continue her campaign.

Her secret was soon out. At the Battle of Ramillies in 1706, a French musket ball fractured her skull and the surgeon who performed the life-saving trepanning operation on her, also discovered her secret. When her commanding officer was informed, he took the news astonishingly well – she had, after all, been a dauntless fighter – and allowed her to stay with the regiment, provided she changed back into her female clothes. News of the story also reached the Duke of Marlborough himself, who suggested that Mr and Mrs Walsh should remarry. This splendid occasion was attended by many of the officers, who for once got the chance to kiss a former comrade openly by way of congratulation.

Mrs Walsh now became cook for the regiment but continued to throw down her ladles and take up a musket whenever the opportunity arose. During her further campaigns she lost her husband at the Battle of Taisnières, discovering him only after turning over 200 bodies on the field. A Captain Ross discovered her weeping over Mr Walsh's dead body and claimed it was a sight that touched him more than the loss of so many brave men.

From this incident Mrs Walsh got the nickname that would stay with her for life – Mother Ross.

But if Mother Ross was down she was certainly not out and eleven weeks later she married another soldier, the grenadier Hugh Jones, who was later killed at the siege of St Venant. After this she returned to England, partly because she was pregnant and also perhaps finally tiring of the wars. Here she was already a celebrity and a petition was put before Queen Anne, outlining her twelve years' military service and requesting a pension, which the queen granted. The queen further promised that if the baby Mother Ross was carrying proved to be a boy, he would immediately be given an army commission from the moment of his birth. Mother Ross was furious when she later gave birth to a daughter.

Mother Ross then returned to Ireland and went back into the pub business although she seems to have made no attempt to find her one surviving son, who was now in the workhouse. Another liaison with a soldier followed and, having married this Mr Davies, she followed him to Hereford where his regiment resided. Mr Davies managed to survive longer than her other husbands and was eventually made a pensioner of the Chelsea Hospital. Mother Ross followed him to London and, on their deaths, the two were both buried in the Chelsea hospital cemetery with full military honours.

What was unusual about Custer's laundress?

One of the more peculiar facts about Mrs Nash the laundress is that no one actually knows his real name – a sentence that in itself should raise a few suspicions.

Mrs Nash first comes to prominence in the USA in the 1870s, working in various roles for Custer's 7th Cavalry regiment, then stationed in Fort Abraham Lincoln, Dakota territory, just before their historic defeat at the Battle of the Little Big Horn. Mrs Nash was believed to have originally come from Mexico and started out in life as an oxen driver working in New Mexico. Somehow she had managed to attach herself to the 7th Cavalry in Kentucky and moved with them to Dakota territory, having secured the lucrative job of company laundress.

To be fair there were some unusual aspects to Mrs Nash, as was noted at the time. She insisted on wearing a veil, which seemed excessively modest for the American frontier, and other women found her difficult to get on with, although that might have had as much to do with competition for her money-spinning job. What everyone could agree on was that she was an excellent laundress, a very good midwife and, as three men in turn could attest, a loyal wife.

The first of these three husbands had been a man called Clifford whom she had lived with for five years. After his discharge she remained in the service, taking up with James Nash and keeping his surname even when he left the service, at which point she moved in with Corporal John Noonan, a fellow Mexican. And so Mrs Nash's career continued until, in 1878, she suddenly died while her husband was away from their home in Fort Meade.

One unconfirmed report states that with her dying breath she asked the other women of the fort to bury her immediately without formally preparing the body. As her husband was absent at the time this request was ignored as it was assumed he would surely want to say his goodbyes to his wife. Even if the women had agreed, they could not have prevented the physician in attendance at the fort from examining the body prior to its laying out. This he did and in the process made a discovery that must already have been known to some in the fort. Mrs Nash was a man. Homosexuality was by no means unknown in the US armed forces at this time but the response to it varied from disgust to hilarity. When Corporal Noonan returned, he found not only that his lover was dead but that the whole regiment knew that he had been secretly living with a cross-dressing man. In the face of such open ridicule he deserted and, two days later, shot himself.

How did a Cornish play prevent an invasion?

The sixteenth-century conflicts between Spain and England did not consist solely of large-scale actions such as the Spanish Armada or the continental battles of the Eighty Years War, but often rumbled on at a much lower and more local level.

Just before, and for many years after, the Armada, this took the form of small-scale raiding on the English coast, particularly those furthest west: in other words, Cornwall. Many of these attacks were probably as much the idea of the small bands of privateers prowling the coast as they were a part of a national Spanish strategy, but their effect was significant. Small groups of heavily armed Spanish raiders would sneak ashore, usually under cover of dark, and pillage local villages and towns, slipping away again back to sea long before the militia could be summoned.

But these raiders did not have it all their own way. The customs of the Cornish in the sixteenth century were still very particular to the region. Although the English were doing their best to eradicate the native Cornish tongue, it still survived, as did the mediaeval mystery plays and traditions that had been part of Cornish life for centuries.

So it was that on a summer night in 1587, the year before the Armada, a Spanish crew stole ashore and made their way to Penryn in hope of plunder. As they reached the town it was clear that something was amiss. The streets were deserted. Perhaps the locals had heard their approach and run, as many before them had? But if the Spaniards thought they would therefore have easy pickings, they were very wrong. At that very moment an almighty roar came from the outskirts of the town, accompanied by trumpets and drums. It could only be a veritable army about to descend. The Spaniards turned on their heels and ran.

When they reached their ship they must have counted themselves lucky to have escaped so fiendish a trap, but in fact the citizens of Penryn were still entirely unaware that their town had ever been under threat. That night was the performance of the traditional mystery play of St Sampson and the town had been deserted because everyone was in a barn on the outskirts of town, watching it. But what was the source of the blood-curdling roar? The mystery play was a powerful piece, acted with great gusto, and the roar had come, not from men ready to avenge themselves on the Spaniards, but from the actors and audience cheering wildly at the point in the story when the gates of Gaza fell. Such had been the conviction of cast and spectators that it had been enough to genuinely put the fear of God in the Spanish raiders, who were even then making all speed to safer waters.

What was an Allotment Annie?

There are always those who manage to turn a profit from war, often by less than salubrious means, but few caused as much resentment in the United States during the Second World War as the 'Allotment Annies'.

In wartime, soldiers married their sweethearts very young. With the shadow of a foreign posting hanging over them, and the very real prospect of never returning alive, many an impulsive marriage was contracted, granting a few days of connubial bliss before the horrors of battle that lay ahead.

But the story of these marriages was sometimes less than romantic. The young brides left behind as their men headed off to war received the 'allotment', part of their husband's pay sent directly to them by the government, amounting to $20 a month, rising to $50 when their spouse was posted overseas. For wives unlucky enough to receive the fateful telegram telling them of their husbands' deaths, there was also the small comfort of the $10,000 life insurance policy.

Whilst it was not possible to get rich on one of these, some women realised that, by marrying more than one man, they could make a handsome living. In the confusion of war few people noticed how these women targeted young soldiers, marrying several just before they left for war and living off their allotments. For the Allotment Annies, bigamy was a business.

But it was, of course, not a business without its risks. There was a danger that multiple husbands might find out about each other. What would happen if two returned on leave at the same time? For the more cynical Annies, and those looking for a more handsome return on their investment, the answer was airmen. Aircrew had some of the lowest life expectancies in the forces and espousing a tail gunner was a marriage worth having, not for the $50 a month but the life insurance payout that would no doubt follow in a few months' time.

Not all Annies got away with their crime. Elvira Taylor's duplicity brought the problem to national attention and made her a pariah. She worked out of the US navy base at Norfolk, Virginia, specialising in marrying sailors, who took long tours of duty on small ships in big oceans and hence could generally be expected to keep out of each other's way. An extraordinary coincidence led to her unmasking. Two US sailors drinking in a pub on the south coast of England had got into a fight when one showed the other a photograph of his wife. It turned out that the other sailor had the same photograph and insisted it was *his* wife. Fists flew but once tempers had cooled both men realised that it was not the other man but Elvira who had duped them and they turned her in to the authorities. A check of navy allotments showed that she was also married to four other sailors.

What military faux pas cost Raleigh his head?

One of the more peculiar features of warfare is that it has rules and these rules can mean that a soldier can be just as much in danger from his own people as he is from the enemy, as Sir Walter Raleigh found to his cost.

From 1603, his star was very definitely no longer in the ascendant. With the death of Elizabeth I and the coronation of James I, Raleigh rapidly fell from favour, thanks largely to the whispers of his enemies who persuaded the new king that the old sea dog had been opposed to his accession. His lucrative monopolies were stripped away, there was talk that he had conspired to place Arabella Stuart on the throne and, before long, he wound up in the Tower of London, only being saved from the block by a last-minute reprieve.

It looked like being a sorry end for one of the greatest Elizabethan adventurers but, in 1616, Raleigh received what appeared to be one more chance. Unfortunately, because of the problems of long-distance communication, it would prove to be the final tragedy. Raleigh was released from the Tower to go in search of a fabled city, which today we know as El Dorado. In 1594, Raleigh had come into possession of a Spanish map showing a golden city at the top of the Caroni river in Guiana and had already once been in search of it, writing up a rather exaggerated version of events on his return. Now the prospect of unlimited riches earned him a release to go and discover this city of 'Manoa'.

Raleigh, and the seafarers who sailed with him, had grown up in an era of war with Spain. They had cut their teeth harrying the New World Spanish treasure fleet. Spain and her possessions had provided much of both their fame and their wealth. However, in 1616 things were different. One of James I's first diplomatic successes had been the arrangement in 1604 of a peace with Spain at the Treaty of London, which brought to a close years of unprofitable war for both sides.

Raleigh sailed for the New World with strict instructions not to molest any Spanish concerns. But old habits die hard and one of Raleigh's captains, Lawrence Keymis, found he could not resist temptation. Despite written and verbal orders to lead his party up the Orinoco yet leave the Spanish settlement of San Thomé well alone, news got back some two months later to Raleigh, then off Trinidad, that Keymis had done exactly the opposite. San Thomé had been attacked, the Spanish garrison had been expelled, and the town and fort had been taken by the British. In the days of Elizabeth this would have been cause for celebration but now times had changed. Tragically, Raleigh's eldest son Wat had been killed in the unauthorised attack. The old soldier met the news with the grim realisation that the taking of San Thomé would also prove to be his death warrant.

Walter Raleigh, the most flamboyant, most fearless seaman of the Elizabethan era, returned home to England a broken man. The loss of his son weighed heavily but the prospect of gold for the royal coffers might at least have saved his own life. He arrived back in Plymouth empty-handed – El Dorado had proved a mirage. He also learnt on reaching England that his anti-Spanish friends had gone from office and the king was now a firm favourite with the Spanish ambassador, Diego Sarmiento de Acuña, conde de Gondomar. When Gondomar, unable to contain his fury at news of Raleigh's exploits, burst in on the king he simply shouted 'Piratas' three times and the great sea-captain's fate was sealed. The trumped-up death sentence, originally ordered years earlier, was reinstated and, on 29 October 1618, Sir Walter Raleigh was beheaded in Whitehall, an old warrior brought low by the fortunes of war.

Pack Up Your Troubles

'Good morning; good morning!' the General said
When we met him last week on our way to the line.
Now the soldiers he smiled at are most of 'em dead,
And we're cursing his staff for incompetent swine.
'He's a cheery old card,' grunted Harry to Jack
As they slogged up to Arras with rifle and pack.
But he did for them both by his plan of attack.

Siegfried Sassoon,
'The General',
Counter-Attack and Other Poems (1918)

Which military leader was 'generally understood to be a madman'?

Sir William Erskine was always destined for a life in the army, following in the footsteps of his father, Lieutenant General Sir William Erskine. He first saw action as his father's aide-de-camp during the peculiarly unsuccessful campaigns of the Duke of York in Flanders between 1793 and 1795, whose comings and goings are sometimes said to have given rise to the famous nursery rhyme about the 'Grand Old Duke of York'.

Despite this to-ing and fro-ing Erskine distinguished himself and returned to England for a career in politics, taking up his father's baronetcy and his brother-in-law's seat in parliament. But, whether the fuse had been lit years before and was simply slow-burning, or whether the strains of Westminster politics took their toll, during this period people began to notice a difference in Erskine. At the very best he was becoming unreliable, whilst many thought he was actually going mad.

So it took a certain degree of wilful blindness on the part of the authorities, in the run-up to Wellington's peninsular campaign, to choose Erskine as one of the commanders, but choose him they did. News of the increasingly unpredictable major general's attachment to the expedition excited a certain degree of disbelief in military circles. Some pointed out that he was so short-sighted as to be almost blind, which might prove a handicap for a cavalry officer. One of his own officers added that he was not only a drunkard but incompetent with it.

But it was his state of mind that most concerned Wellington, who was being asked to entrust the lives of soldiers to this man. Desperate to be rid of him, he wrote to Lieutenant Colonel Henry Torrens, the military secretary at the Horse Guards, noting that Erskine was 'generally understood to be a madman'. If he had hoped that such blunt words might drive the danger home, he was very much mistaken. Torrens, ever the optimist, replied: 'No doubt he is sometimes a little mad, but in his lucid intervals he is an uncommonly clever fellow; and I trust he may have no fit during the campaign,' before adding, ominously, 'though he looked a little wild before he embarked'.

Indeed, Erskine was a little wild. In Spain he proved brave but reckless, charging his men into fog banks in one incident that nearly led to the destruction of the Light Division. He also proved rather inept at siege warfare, on one occasion allowing a convoy into a city that he was supposedly besieging and on another allowing the besieged army out. By 1812 his growing insanity had become evident even to the High Command back in Britain and Erskine was finally relieved of duty, although he would never live to see home again. On 13 February 1813, at Brozas, while in bed with a fever, he threw himself from the bedroom window to his death in what was described as 'a fit of delirium'. One story has it that, as he lay dying on the ground, he asked a passer-by, 'Why did I do that?'

Why did General Hajianestis play dead?

The Graeco-Turkish war, fought between 1919 and 1922, was a particularly unsatisfactory affair (for Greece at least). Its chief intention, as Britain had promised, was to give Greece more territory at the expense of the now defunct Ottoman empire, but it ended up with Greece giving up all the territory it had gained from the First World War.

Whilst blame for this humiliating reverse cannot be entirely laid at the door of one person, the Greek general Georgios Hajianestis certainly didn't help. Hajianestis was fifty-six years old at the outbreak of hostilities and had been a brave and brilliant soldier in his youth. In recent years, however, a certain mental deterioration had been widely noted in him; indeed, the British prime minister, David Lloyd George, considered him a 'mental weakling'. Ominously, this didn't stand in the way of his appointment as supreme commander of Greece's army in the war.

Initially the advantage lay with Greece after its occupation of

Smyrna, followed by further gains down the Aegean coast of Anatolia, greatly increasing Greece's coastline. In 1920 their star began to wane. King Alexander of Greece was bitten by two of his pet monkeys while walking in the Royal Gardens, developed septicaemia and died. As a result the Greek people had to decide whether to opt for a republic or for the return of King Constantine, whose marked pro-German sympathies in the First World War had eventually forced him to retire to Switzerland.

Amid this confusion the Greek troops in Anatolia had a more pressing problem. While they were taking territory in Asia Minor, their commander, Georgios Hajianestis, was nowhere to be seen. In fact he had not even gone ashore with his army but had chosen to direct the campaign from the safety of a yacht moored off Smyrna. As a defence against reality, this move proved illusory. Aboard ship, the pressure of political changes at home, plus the increasingly strong defence being put up by the Turks under Kemal Atatürk, were taking their toll on him and he spent most of his time in bed, complaining of neuralgia. This soon gave way to a more pronounced delusion when he began announcing that he couldn't get up to run the war as his legs might snap. This, he told his bemused staff, was because his legs were made of sugar – or sometimes, he would claim, they were glass.

Needless to say, word of the supreme commander's unusual affliction soon leaked out and morale among the Greek troops plummeted. And so the tide of war turned.

The final battle occurred at Dumlupinar, between 26 and 30 August 1922. It degenerated into a rout in which the Greek army was driven back 250 miles, first to Smyrna and then out of Turkey altogether. There was still just time, however, for Hajianestis to bequeath the world one more moment of military lunacy. Instead of organising the retreat and evacuation of his men, the general decided to play dead, refusing to be woken up, on the grounds that if he was dead he was relieved of his command and bore no responsibility for the debacle.

Unfortunately for Hajianestis, the authorities back in Greece did indeed hold him responsible, despite his very apparent mental illness. He was tried for high treason and executed in 1922.

What happened when the British army stopped for tea?

The First World War landings at Gallipoli were not quite the unmitigated success that the British had hoped for, due in part to a series of extremely poor decisions in planning and executing the attack, not least of which was picking a highly unfortunate moment to take tea.

The strategy for the 1915 assault was to force a landing on the Gallipoli peninsula in the Dardanelles, securing the coast so that the British navy could move in and seize Constantinople. In theory, it would knock the pro-German Ottoman empire out of the war at a stroke and open a sea route to Russia. Initially it had been thought that it might be possible to do this with sea power alone, using British and French ships that were considered too outdated to oppose the German fleet. This attack began on 19 February, with the main bombardment from eighteen battleships and a host of destroyers following on 18 March. The plan went awry when the minesweepers employed to clear the channel of mines were driven back in the face of artillery from the cliffs. Consequently the British fleet steamed into mine-infested waters, with predictable results, including the sinking of the battleships HMS *Ocean* and HMS *Irresistible*.

After this the Allied forces retired to think up a new course of action. Clearly a ground force would be needed to knock out the artillery on the coastline but the huge naval bombardment had rather given the game away and Turkish troops were now flooding into the area. A further six-week delay while the British prepared plans for the landings gave the Ottomans plenty of time to re-inforce their line. The intelligence information about enemy troop numbers, gathered by Lieutenant T.E. Lawrence (later famous as Lawrence of Arabia), thus became entirely worthless.

In spite of this the operation was ordered to go ahead. In charge was General Sir Ian Hamilton who planned a main attack by Australian and New Zealand (ANZAC) forces at Gaba Tepe, with a British attack at Cape Helles on the southern tip of the peninsula, plus two diversionary attacks by the French and the British to draw Turkish troops away.

There were a number of flaws in these tactics. First, Hamilton was denied the night-time landing he had asked for as the navy refused, claiming it would be too difficult. Second, he was having trouble maintaining contact with his own staff, in part because he had left his entire logistical brigade 700 miles away in Cairo, and in part because of his insistence on operating out of the flagship HMS *Queen Elizabeth* whilst his operations staff were on a separate transport ship. As the admiral could not always move his battleship to where the transport was, this made for rather chaotic communications.

Despite all these setbacks the landings took place on 25 April and, although most of the troops had never been in an amphibious landing before (indeed, many had never even been in a battle), for a while success seemed possible, provided it came quickly. However, events soon began once again to take a turn for the worse. Many of the ANZAC forces landed on the wrong beach and before they could reach their goal, the hill of Chunuk Bair, it was seized by Turks under the command of Mustafa Kemal (later Kemal Atatürk, first President of Turkey). Meanwhile the British 29th Division successfully executed the Cape Helles landings to divert attention from the ANZACs but suffered terrible casualties on two of their landing beaches.

However, at Y beach, an isolated spot that the Turks had considered an unlikely point of attack, the 2,000-strong British force encountered only four enemy soldiers. The men quickly scaled the cliff and, through the smoke and flame of battle raging on the beaches around them, saw the little village of Krithia ahead of them – the vital strategic gain necessary to take the peninsula.

The problem was that no one had thought about the next move. General Hamilton was on his battleship, far out to sea, and most of the other commanders were rather busy fighting. So two officers from the Y beach assault reportedly walked into a near-deserted Krithia and had a look round. They then returned to their men, sat them down on the cliff top and decided to let the unit have a cup of tea and do a bit of sunbathing.

During that tea break the initiative was lost. The Turks received orders to rush reinforcing troops to the village. By mid-afternoon the British troops were no longer sipping tea, but had been driven back to Y beach and were digging in for a long and bloody siege that would only end with their evacuation on 8 January 1916, over eight months later. In that time nearly 100,000 soldiers from both sides would be killed and another 237,000 wounded.

What was the mutiny at Sandhurst?

Sandhurst Royal Military College is the training ground of the British army officer and as such is the place where duty, drill and obedience are drummed into the future leaders of the army. So it is perhaps surprising to find that it has also been a hotbed of mutiny.

One such very British mutiny occurred in 1902 when disciplinary action was taken against the whole body of cadets over a series of mysterious fires in the compound, of which the officers-to-be declared themselves completely innocent. Roused by this unjust treatment, the cadets of 'C' company decided to mutiny, beginning by gathering on the main steps of the college and toasting every Boer general they could think of.

Things then became a little livelier. One group went to the governor's house, stood outside the window where the governor was holding a dinner party and began singing the sorts of Sandhurst songs that were never meant for delicate ears. The others rampaged through the grounds, bending lampposts and hurling everything movable, including the cannons in the courtyard, into the lake.

At this point one bright spark hit upon the very height of revolution – the one thing guaranteed to upset the establishment. They would all leave the compound without permission and go to Camberley fête. So it was that the cadets, in full mess dress, swept out of Sandhurst and into the fête, without even stopping to pay the entrance fee. Whilst some mutineers steal ships and others start revolutions, the Sandhurst mutineers contented themselves with riding on the merry-go-round and the swings.

In face of this very British mutiny the response was equally British. Following another mystery fire, 'C' company were all initially rusticated – that is, sent down from college. Sometime later, letters arrived at the desperadoes' homes, asking them to attend personal interviews at the War Office with the commander-in-chief of the British army, Field Marshal the Earl Roberts. He had a quiet word with each cadet and made them swear that they had no idea who was starting the fires. In return for this, they were reinstated as cadets and the end-of-term examinations they had missed were marked as 'passed'. And that was the end of the Sandhurst mutiny.

How did Frederick the Great keep the lights out?

Many of the stories told of Frederick the Great play up his great love for his troops (see page 43), as well as his sympathy for and understanding of the lot of the common soldier. According to the *Life of Frederick the Second, King of Prussia* by Jean-Charles Laveaux, published in 1789, he could also prove a strict disciplinarian, finding his own unique way of ensuring a soldier didn't ignore his orders twice.

Laveaux records: 'In the first war of Silesia, wishing to make some alterations in his camp, during the night, he forbade every person, under pain of death, to keep, after a certain hour, a fire or other light in his tent.'

Frederick would not tolerate any plan of his being compromised by disobedience and so, after the appointed hour, he went round in person to check that there were no lights showing. As he reached the tent of one Captain Zietern, however, he saw a flame and, on entering, found the man just finishing sealing a letter to his wife. The light from the sealing wax was only dim and Captain Zietern, fearful for his future and deeply in love, was not unusual in wanting to write home. But orders were orders. Laveaux takes up the conversation:

'What are you doing there? says the king; Do not you know the orders? Zietern throws himself on his knees, and begs pardon, but neither could nor would attempt to deny his fault.'

If Zietern hoped this display of honest contrition would be enough, he was mistaken. The king ordered him to sit down again, told him to unseal his letter and add a few words to the end that he would dictate. He then dictated, 'I shall perish tomorrow on a scaffold.' Laveaux finishes the story: 'Zietern wrote them, and, the next day, was executed.'

How did a soldier gain his life but lose his wife?

A rather similar tale to that of Captain Zeitern, but with a more bitter-sweet ending, is told by Richard Steele in an article for the *Tatler* published on Thursday, 27 April 1710.

Steele recalls a story from the English Civil War concerning a soldier who had been taken prisoner by the enemy. The lot of a prisoner of war during civil conflicts is often a very unhappy one as, being of the same nation but on a different side, the prisoner can easily be accused of treachery and hence executed. This was to be the fate of this captured corporal who, having received a sentence of execution, had to write to his wife to tell her the news.

Knowing he was to be executed the next day, but that the message would only reach his wife after he had died, he had something of a problem with his tenses when he came to write the letter. Should he refer to himself as alive – which he clearly was at the time of writing – or dead, as he would surely be at the time it was read? Rather confusingly, he chose a middle course and wrote:

> Dear Wife,
>
> Hoping you are in good Health, as I am at this present Writing. This is to let you know, that Yesterday, between the Hours of Eleven and Twelve, I was hanged, drawn and quartered. I died very penitently, and every Body thought my Case very hard. Remember me kindly to my poor Fatherless Children.
>
> W.B.

However, as luck would have it, before the terrible day dawned the corporal was rescued by his own men and it was he who watched his captors meet their deaths the following morning. It was too late to intercept the letter to his wife telling of his imminent demise and by the time he returned home from the war she had remarried. As she had written proof in his own hand that he was dead, he chose never to interfere in her new marital arrangements.

What did the Spanish and French do to keep warm in Denmark?

The first thought of any army should be to provide for its immediate defence, whether in a camp or a castle. The second thought should be to ensure that that defence remains intact. Ideally.

In September 1808 these thoughts were far from the minds of the 30,000 Spanish and French soldiers sent to Denmark, which had recently taken sides with Napoleon in his continental wars. For the Spaniards in particular, their arrival at the dilapidated castle of Koldinghus in a winter that was icy even by Danish standards was particularly unwelcome. It was, frankly, too cold.

News soon reached the French commander in the castle, Jean-Baptiste Bernadotte, that the structure itself was in danger from the activities of the Spanish contingent. In an attempt to stay warm, the troops were throwing whatever they could find, including the furniture, into braziers and burners, lighting fires wherever they could find something to burn. Bernadotte probably didn't feel the cold too badly – he later became king of Sweden and Norway so one assumes not – but he appreciated the difficulty. In response he hired three pairs of local builders (since they understood buildings), each working in shifts as firewatchers, to ensure the safety of his castle.

The idea might have been sound but the sheer quantity of very cold Spaniards in such a small space, together with a slight lack of application on the part of the Danish firewatchers, would lead to disaster. It was late on the night of 29 March 1808 when the smell of smoke was first reported but this was put down to a particular fireplace, known to smoke if the wind was in the wrong direction. Besides, there were two firewatchers on duty who would have noticed anything out of the ordinary. Or at least there should have been. At around 2 or 3 a.m. Søren Weile had gone home, allegedly to 'get some refreshments', but he had 'forgotten' to come back. His fellow watcher, a carpenter called Beiker, hadn't turned up at all as he was ill, but he had omitted to send a message to the castle to tell them he needed replacing.

It was actually a remarkably calm and composed maid who woke the mistress of the castle, Mrs Hviid, at 4.30 a.m. with the words, 'Do not take fright, but the castle is burning,' and, sure enough, she was right. Pandemonium ensued as the troops were sent to the nearby lake to fetch water, only to report back that the lake was frozen and they couldn't get any. By now the fire had taken hold and by first light nearly the whole castle, with the exception of the Giant Tower, had been lost.

This was not bad news for everyone, however. On 2 May, Spain rebelled against France and the chilly Spanish soldiers were shipped back home to warmer climes by the British to assist with the war there. Nor did the firewatchers suffer. Despite their negligence, no one was brought to book for the fire. Within weeks much of the collapsed stonework had mysteriously disappeared from the ruined site – smuggled away by those same local builders to find a home in new construction work.

How did the Romans 'sting' Boudicca?

There was a lot more to the Roman method of conquest than simply sending in the legions to overawe and oppress subject nations. Behind the military might lay a neat little trick of apparent rapprochement, followed by a ruthless financial takeover, as unwary subject kings would discover to their cost.

One such king was Prasutagus of the British Iceni tribe. After the Roman invasion of AD 43 some of the old-guard aristocracy, like himself, had done rather well. Instead of being kicked out and replaced with Roman administrators, they had been made 'client kings' with much of their prestige intact. Now they had the added advantage of access to the luxuries of the Roman world and the protection of the Roman army. It was a good deal for the Romans too as it allowed time for Roman ways to filter into local societies without stirring up trouble by removing their old rulers.

But what Rome was really doing was getting its feet under the table. Being made a client king was really an illusion although no one had told Prasutagus. He had, in many ways, never had it so good and the Iceni aristocracy, along with leading members of many other tribes, freely indulged in all that the Roman world had to offer. Of course this cost money but, as the elite of society, they were best placed to find this and if they ever ran short there was plenty of Roman credit available.

So, as Prasutagus neared death, his thoughts turned to the future of his people. As far as he could see things looked bright. He had a feisty wife, called Boudicca, and two daughters who could inherit his kingdom. Obviously the Romans would want something too so he'd leave half of his kingdom to the emperor, by way of a thank-you. And so he died happy.

The truth behind Roman conquest now emerged. What Prasutagus hadn't realised was that the benefits of client kingship were for one generation only. With the Romans now firmly installed and the people apparently quiet, they didn't want half a kingdom; they wanted all of it. And so they precipitated a banking crisis. Back in Rome those wealthy senators who had been lending Prasutagus and his friends money to live the high life – a group that included the orator Seneca – suddenly called in their debts. Of course the Iceni couldn't pay so in the ensuing 'credit crunch' the Roman fiscal procurator stepped in and began seizing the assets of the kingdom.

Boudicca complained, as you might expect, but was whipped for her trouble and her daughters raped. Unlike Iron Age British society, the Romans didn't have a very high opinion of female rulers. So began the Iceni revolt that would lead to the destruction of the Roman cities of Londinium (London), Camulodunum (Colchester) and Verulamium (St Albans), the death of Boudicca herself and, finally, the reluctant assimilation of the Iceni into the Roman world.

How did Lord Falkland make an exit?

Lord Falkland was one of Charles I's more moderate supporters during the English Civil War, serving as his principal Secretary of State after the Battle of Edgehill. It was a difficult situation for the very rational Falkland, trying to pick a path between the extremists in both Royalist and Parliamentarian camps, both of whom he deeply distrusted.

By the summer of 1643 it was clear to his friends that the rigours of war, as well as the apparent refusal of both sides to behave reasonably, was taking its toll on Falkland. According to his close friend Edward Hyde, he would sit sighing over the futility of the conflict, occasionally punctuating his sighs with a shrill shout of, 'Peace, peace'.

According to the somewhat more scurrilous John Aubrey, around this time Falkland's long-term mistress Mrs Moray also died. As she was 'the one whom he loved above all creatures', this and the ceaseless fighting finally turned his mind. If there is one thing a civil war does provide ample opportunity for, it's death, and so Lord Falkland chose to end it all with an unusual suicide.

His initial attempts to get himself killed proved fruitless and, despite doing his damnedest to appear in all the most dangerous positions during the siege of Gloucester, he emerged entirely unscathed. However, the first Battle of Newbury on 20 September supplied the opening he had been looking for. Volunteering to join the first rank of Lord Byron's regiment, he told his friends that 'he was weary of the times, and foresaw much misery to his own country, and did believe he should be out of it ere night'. Then, picking a gap in a hedge into which Parliamentarian musketeers were pouring fire from both sides, he rode straight for the opening, receiving a fatal shot almost instantly. He was buried in Great Tew where he had lived before the war, with his friends still unsure whether his death counted as a heroic demise in the face of the enemy or suicide. It was left to John Aubrey to note that 'there is no great wit without an admixture of madness.'

Shot in the foot

They couldn't hit an elephant at this distance.

Major General John Sedgwick (shortly before being shot dead at the Battle of Spotsylvania Court House), 9 May 1864

What was the most dangerous part of Sir Arthur Aston's body?

Sir Arthur Aston was not an especially popular commander during the English Civil War and not only the enemy, but also many of his men, often wished him dead. Nonetheless, few can have imagined that he would eventually be killed by a part of his own body. Aston's overt Catholicism and reputation for brusqueness had made Charles I wary of employing him in the opening stages of the conflict but he was eventually given a commission, if only to prevent the Parliamentarians from hiring him. So began a period of wildly varying fortunes for Sir Arthur.

As governor of Reading during the Edgehill campaign, Aston got off to a flying start in alienating both the townsfolk and his troops by blowing up the abbey to provide stone to fortify the civic walls – which they were then forced to build. These preparations proved ineffective and in April 1643 the town fell to the Earl of Essex. The humiliation of surrendering was delegated to a junior officer as Aston had reputedly been hit by a falling brick and rendered speechless. This added to his unpopularity as it was widely believed that there was nothing really wrong with him, other than an unwillingness to admit his own defeat.

Nevertheless, by August he was governor of Oxford, an appointment ordered by the royal family themselves. Here he made no more effort to rub along with his people, becoming a byword for arrogance and bullying – even beating up the mayor on one occasion. With friends like this, the Royalists really didn't have time for a civil war as well and so it was to great sighs of relief that the news came through in September that Sir Arthur had fallen from his horse and broken his leg. The break later turned gangrenous and the leg was amputated, providing the perfect excuse for retiring the cantankerous old soldier on a large pension, despite his protestations.

So Aston lived in relative anonymity until 1649 when, regardless of his less than diplomatic record, Prince Rupert recommended him as governor of the port of Drogheda. By now Charles I was dead and the hopes of a quick restoration of the monarchy rested on Ireland, although it was clear that Cromwell would go to any lengths to prevent this. In September, Cromwell laid siege to the port and demanded that Sir Arthur surrender his garrison. Keen not to repeat the humiliation of Reading, Aston made one last diplomatic blunder and refused, in the face of overwhelming odds. On 10 September, Cromwell's men entered the town, swearing to give no quarter to the belligerent garrison and leading to a massacre. Arthur Aston, never the most well-liked of men, was quickly located and beaten to death with his own wooden leg.

How were the Venetians saved by the wind?

By 1849 the Austrian army had got over its fear of balloons (see page 99) and was beginning to think about embracing this new technology. Certainly the army needed some way of turning the tide of the war, having been expelled from Venice (which they controlled) by Daniele Manin who had declared a new Venetian republic.

Now camped around the city, they had been trying to starve the Venetians out but her citizens were proving rather resistant. Despite chronic shortages of food and other supplies, they had sworn 'Resistance at all costs!' which seemed quite clear.

It was into this situation that the idea of aerial bombing was first floated by Austrian artillery captain and inventor, Franz von Uchatius. The Austrians had become rather taken with the concept of deploying balloons in warfare but Uchatius wondered whether they could be used for more than reconnaissance. What if they were used to bomb the city? To the Austrian High Command it seemed like an excellent idea and 200 small paper Montgolfière balloons were ordered for the purpose.

Reasoning that large manned balloons would obviously make a very easy target from the ground, the Austrians came up with an automatic system where each small, unmanned, and hence hard to hit, balloon carried an explosive mechanism attached to a timing device that released it over the city after a given period of time.

The idea seemed foolproof. On 12 July 1849 'pilot' balloons were filled and sent over the city to gauge the wind speed and direction for the bombing run. With a course successfully plotted, the balloon bombing fleet was filled with hot air, the timers were set and the grenades primed before being floated off across the lagoon in the direction of the city. Venice was about to be the first metropolis ever to be threatened by aerial bombing.

At this point an obvious but overlooked flaw made itself rather evident. Some of the Austrian solders began noticing that the little balloons seemed to be getting closer, not further away, as indeed they were. The wind had changed direction and the bombers were heading straight back over the Austrian lines.

What ensued was a scene of some considerable confusion. Austrian troops began firing at the diminutive balloons in a desperate attempt to hit them before their timers released their grenades. This of course was rather difficult as the balloons were so small. Even once they had shot them down, there was the problem of disposing of the grenades. Thus it was that the first aerial bombing mission in history had the singular effect of driving back the very army that had launched it.

Fortunately for the Austrians, most of the balloons drifted harmlessly overhead, randomly bombing fields, lakes and whatever else happened to be beneath as they floated off in a variety of directions. Traditional tactics were hastily reverted to and, on 24 August, the Venetians, now entirely without food or ammunition, surrendered.

Who said, 'Well, don't worry about it'?

It is highly dangerous to wait for the impossible to happen since, because it's impossible, you're taken a little off your guard when it happens. In warfare rarely has this been more the case than in the hours before the Japanese raid on Pearl Harbor, Hawaii, on Sunday, 7 December 1941.

Although many in the US government expected war, few expected such astonishing boldness as the Japanese displayed in attacking the US Pacific fleet in harbour. The first clue came at 3.42 a.m. when a US minesweeper reported seeing a Japanese midget submarine outside the port. She alerted the destroyer USS *Ward*, which initially failed to confirm the contact but eventually sank one midget sub, possibly the same one, nearly three hours later.

By this time the Japanese aircraft of the carrier fleet were already in the air and headed for Hawaii. But it was still not too late for the Americans to act. They had installed long-range, early-warning radar systems on the Hawaiian islands as early as December 1939 to guard against an attack from the Pacific. Only days earlier, one of these six mobile systems had been moved to Opana Point where, on the morning of 7 December, the early shift was being taken by Private Joseph L. Lockard and Private George Elliot. Having only recently been moved, the radar was still officially in 'training' mode and not operational. The men were just practising with the equipment when they noticed a very large signal at 7.02 a.m., two minutes after they were supposed to switch the system off. They duly called in to the Information Center at Fort Shafter, only to find that the centre staff were all at breakfast, as the radar was officially 'offline' from seven o'clock. Instead they were routed through to the sole person on duty, First Lieutenant Kermit Tyler.

Neither Tyler nor the operators had ever seen a radar signal that big before but Tyler had heard that a flight of sixteen B17 Flying Fortresses was due in that day. He also knew from a friend in a bomber section that local radio stations played continuous Hawaiian music when flights were inbound to help guide them in. As he had heard Hawaiian music on the radio on his way into the centre that morning, he assumed the blip was the B17s, which were due in on a very similar heading to that in the radar report.

Poor Lieutenant Tyler then issued one of the most infamous remarks in military history, telling the callers, 'Well, don't worry about it.'

Nevertheless, the radar operators continued to monitor the incoming blips until they disappeared in interference in the shadow of a mountain. At 7.48 a.m. the first wave of Japanese planes attacked, taking the Americans completely by surprise. Five US battleships and two destroyers would be sunk and many other ships damaged. Altogether, 1,247 military personnel and thirty-five civilians were killed.

Kermit Tyler, who fatefully told the radar operators to ignore the incoming Japanese planes, cannot take all the blame of course. The early-warning personnel seemed to believe that it would be impossible for anyone to attack them while they were still training, thereby ignoring the clearest warning they could ever have had. Tyler was heavily criticised in the ensuing investigation but later heroically led the 44th Fighter Squadron to Guadalcanal, retiring after the war as a lieutenant colonel.

Who was followed around by a barrel of whisky?

Nathan G. 'Shanks' Evans was one of the US Confederate Army's more colourful leaders – a knock-kneed (hence the nickname) loose cannon with a reputation for combining foul-mouthed drunken insubordination with considerable military success.

Evans, a Southerner from South Carolina, had originally been a captain in the US 2nd Cavalry but had gone over to the Confederate cause in 1861. At West Point he had been famously argumentative, attacking not only those who disagreed with him but even those who stood silently by. His extraordinary conviction seemed to mark him out as an ideal war leader at the outbreak of the American Civil War.

It was obvious from the start, however, that Evans would fight the war in his own unique way. At the First Battle of Bull Run he was credited with turning the tables on the Union Army and driving it back to Washington, DC. During the battle his bravery was widely acclaimed as he was seen to dart from position to position, giving orders to his troops, regardless of the danger to himself. It was also noted that this exemplary courage was not entirely drawn from his own inner resources. As he ran around the front line, dodging bullets, it was noticed that his Prussian orderly followed on behind, a small one-gallon drum (a barrelito) of whisky on his back. When Evans arrived at a dangerous position, he would get his orderly to pour him another stiffener from the barrel before once more risking life and limb. By the end of the battle he was clearly quite drunk, but since his men were triumphant Evans's alcoholic helper was quietly ignored.

Evans himself did not make any attempt to hide his prodigious drinking. Following another magnificent success at the Battle of Ball's Bluff, there was little his High Command could do but promote him to brigadier general, even though he had been reported to have been 'drinking freely' during the battle. And so the war's most heroic alcoholic stumbled on, shadowed by his faithful barrel of whisky.

Bad luck, or perhaps whisky, finally caught up with Evans at the Battle of Kinston. Although his men were greatly outnumbered, it was expected that he would manage a controlled retreat. Instead he found himself with half his troops on the wrong side of a burning bridge (which he himself had set alight) and withdrawal turned to rout. Evans was accused by some of his own officers of being drunk – or at least too drunk – and he was tried by a military court. Much to everyone's surprise, however, he was exonerated. Nonetheless, Shanks's character had been dealt a decisive blow. His men, to whom he would issue whisky in buckets, were beginning, perhaps rightly, to share his reputation as heavy drinkers and became known as the 'Tramp Brigade'.

Evans was eventually relieved of his command by General Beauregard and, after an injury in a riding accident, he never took to the field again, not even when drunk. After the war he got a job worthy of a courageous dipsomaniac and became a headmaster.

How did 'Beast' Butler upset the belles?

One of the most delicate jobs in a war is managing an occupied city. The inhabitants are certainly not glad to see you, your own forces may be none too warmly inclined towards those who have been fighting them, and no one yet knows whether the current state of affairs is permanent or could be turned on its head at any moment.

Maintaining calm in this situation requires great diplomacy and that is exactly what Major General Benjamin F. Butler did not bring to the situation. In April 1862, amid the fury of the American Civil War, Butler took the Deep South city of New Orleans from the Confederates. For many in the city it seemed a terrible humiliation and some of the female inhabitants in particular took to goading their Union occupiers in the hope of persuading the now passive and paroled Confederate troops in the town to revolt.

The women of New Orleans proved rather good at goading, as it happened, and Butler began receiving reports of his men being spat at in the street, of the ladies of the French Quarter crossing the road to avoid them, of heckling, and of the brazen singing of Confederate songs. One unfortunate Yankee, Captain David C. Farragut, even had a full chamber pot emptied over his head.

If this wasn't what Butler expected from Southern belles, his response is certainly not what they expected from an officer and a gentleman. General Order no. 28, issued on 15 May, stated:

> As the officers and soldiers of the United States have been subjected to repeated insults from the women (calling themselves ladies) of New Orleans, in return for the most scrupulous non-interference and courtesy on our part, it is ordered that hereafter

> when any female shall, by word, gesture, or movement, insult or show contempt for any officer or soldier of the United States, she shall be regarded and held liable to be treated as a woman of the town plying her avocation.

In other words, any woman who was rude to a soldier would be treated like a prostitute, which at that time meant being imprisoned on Ship Island.

The order caused outrage, not just among the ladies of New Orleans, but in the Union High Command as well as the Confederate. There were even protests from as far away as France and England. The real prostitutes of New Orleans also showed their disapproval by sticking pictures of Butler to the inside of their chamber pots (see page 83 for the further dangers of annoying prostitutes during the US Civil War).

The response from Butler's commanders was swift. His outrageous suggestion that all Confederate women were effectively whores – combined with his illegal seizure of $800,000 deposited in the Dutch consulate, and his false imprisonment of the French champagne magnate Charles Heidsieck – led to his being removed from command. For the rest of a rather undistinguished war, Butler, who had previously been nicknamed 'Spoons' – supposedly for his habit of stealing the silverware from the Confederate homes he stayed in – was dogged by the new nickname 'Beast Butler'.

What was MacCarthy's nasty surprise?

Brigadier General Sir Charles MacCarthy was rather enlightened, as nineteenth-century British colonial governors went. A regular correspondent with William Wilberforce, the great anti-slavery campaigner, he took a keen interest in the well-being of the people of Sierra Leone whom he governed, providing schooling for the children of those captured by slavers, and settlements for freed slaves. It is therefore something of a shame that his skull should end up one day being used as a cup by an Ashanti ruler.

How he came to this sorry state is a tale of bad luck, but most of all bad planning. In late 1823, MacCarthy sided with the Fanti people in their struggles with the Ashanti, declaring war on the latter. Setting off with around 500 men in one of four expeditions designed to converge on and overwhelm the Ashanti warriors, MacCarthy unfortunately stumbled upon a 10,000-strong enemy army before he could join up with the others. He had, however, been told that the enemy contained many disaffected elements who might defect or at least withdraw. As a result, he took the unusual step of ordering the national anthem to be played very loudly, in the process not only giving away his exact position but also discovering that his intelligence had been wildly mistaken.

The two armies now came together on opposite banks of the Pra river, neither side trying to cross the eighteen-metre-wide stream but instead firing from the relative safety of the banks. As the day wore on, it became increasingly clear to MacCarthy that he could hold off the vastly superior Ashanti force only while he had enough ammunition to keep them on the other side of the river. His men reported that they were running short of both ball and powder. The situation was becoming increasingly critical. News came from the rear of his party that many of the bearers bringing up supplies had run away at the sound of gunfire, making supplies very limited. Soon his Fanti recruits were shouting to him that they were out of powder. This was unfortunate as the Fanti could be understood by the Ashanti, who now realised that they could press home their advantage.

In a last desperate bid, MacCarthy ordered his troops drawn up and the reserve supplies of ammunition distributed, which consisted of just one barrel of powder and one of shot. It was in this final, anguished moment, as the barrels were opened, that he realised his ultimate fatal error. In the confusion in the rear of his company, the last barrels brought forward were not what he had hoped for. Opening them, he discovered they were filled not with powder but with macaroni, scarcely an effective substitute. One report says that MacCarthy now gave the order to retreat and then shot himself. Others claim he was captured and beheaded by the Ashanti. Only twenty men escaped with their lives.

What was Aleksei Kuropatkin's bright idea?

Aleksei Kuropatkin did not enter the First World War with an unblemished reputation. His career in the Russian army had started well enough, his graduation from the famous Pavlovsky Military School being followed by successful campaigns in the conquest of Turkestan. In the Russo-Turkish War he had been promoted to a staff position and by 1882 was a major general at the age of just thirty-four.

After a spell as minister of war, his downfall began in 1904 when he was placed in charge of all the Russian Far-Eastern forces in the Russo-Japanese War. A series of defeats ensued, including the disastrous Battle of Mukden, after which it was reported that two of his generals had had a fight on the railway station there. Realising that the situation was now beyond his control, he did at least have the decency to ask to be replaced, an offer that the Russian High Command seized upon with alacrity.

As he had been widely criticised for his lack of decisiveness and organisation during the campaign, the future looked rather bleak for Kuropatkin until the advent of the First World War brought him back to the reluctant notice of the Russian High Command. In the autumn of 1915 he was given command of a grenadier corps despite attempts by the tsar to prevent this. Seeing the appointment as his final chance to put the record straight, Kuropatkin developed a plan to demonstrate his true military genius.

During the Russo-Turkish War, back in the days when his military record was unblemished, he had come across a useful new piece of technology – the searchlight. This had enabled the Russians to light areas around their encampments at night, hence preventing attacks under cover of darkness. Kuropatkin had been impressed by these intense lights and now saw another potential way of using them. He suggested that, during an advance, searchlights should be shone directly at the enemy. This would not only illuminate their positions but would also dazzle them, allowing his men to approach without being fired on.

It should not take too much thought to work out the logical flaw in this plan, but sadly neither Kuropatkin nor his staff seem to have hit upon it. And so in early 1916 the grenadiers advanced on the German lines with huge, dazzling searchlights behind them. From the German perspective, every single Russian soldier was perfectly outlined by the lights and 8,000 were shot dead as they moved forward. Kuropatkin staggered on until July 1916 when he again resigned. He ended his days teaching at the agricultural school that he had founded in Pskov.

Whose desire to kill a tommy nearly killed him?

Many years after the end of the American Revolutionary War, a number of old soldiers applied for state pensions. Their statements to the court concerning their service reveal many of the smaller details of the conflict that have often escaped the notice of historians. The statement of John Chaney in particular, given on 29 March 1833 before the circuit court of Green County, Indiana, records one unfortunate moment of hubris.

Chaney was camped with William Washington's dragoons at Saluda Old Town, just 100 yards away from a British sentry post. The temptation to take a potshot at this lone sentinel was almost irresistible but the brigade captain urged restraint. In particular, one Billy Lunsford, who was due to end his military service the following day and head home for Virginia, was insistent that he would 'have it to tell that he had killed one damned British son of a bitch'. The captain replied that there would be no tactical point in killing the man and, as he was only doing his duty, it seemed perhaps a shade churlish to creep up behind him and shoot him when he wasn't looking.

Lunsford was determined to have the tommy's scalp, however,

and, disobeying orders, he sneaked off in the gathering gloom of evening to bring down the British sentry. Aware that he might be spotted, he decided to get within range of the man by going on all fours and grunting like a pig, presumably in the hope that the sentry would think he was exactly that.

At this point his scheme miscarried. Whether the sentry noticed there was a rebel creeping through the bushes grunting, or simply thought that there was a decent meal snuffling about in the undergrowth, he took aim and fired. Considering the failing light, it was a remarkably good shot, passing straight through Lunsford's abdomen and making him squeal all the louder. This quickly brought reinforcements to the British position and Lunsford was taken prisoner, hence scuppering his plans both to 'bag a Briton' and to go home. Fortunately for him, the British surgeon managed to save his life and he survived.

Who threw away a fortune escaping?

On 5 January 1809, the British army was in retreat from Villa Franca. The Napoleonic wars were in full swing and Napoleon himself had just entered the peninsula with 200,000 troops. In response, the British commander, Sir John Moore, was making a tactical withdrawal to the ports of Vigo and Corunna, ready for an evacuation of his forces.

The winter of 1809 was particularly harsh and the retreat rapidly turned from an orderly withdrawal into a shambolic flight. Lieutenant Colonel Charles Cadell of the 28th regiment noted one typical disaster in his *Narratives of the Campaigns of the 28th Regiment since their Return from Egypt in 1802*. He records how, as the army retreated, they came across an abandoned baggage train. The exhausted and dispirited soldiers were allowed to take what supplies they needed from this, while the rest was destroyed to prevent it falling into French hands. But one piece of baggage proved slightly more contentious. The 28th, acting as rearguards, came across two bullock carts loaded with silver dollars – presumably pay for troops. The animals that had been hauling the load were exhausted from being driven too hard and could not continue, so a decision had to be made about what to do with all this cash.

Obviously the soldiers had a very good idea about what to do with it – they wanted to keep it – but Sir John Moore was concerned that in scrabbling for the money they would lose vital time and, as their retreat was being harried all the way, they were likely to be ambushed. He therefore took the highly unpopular decision to have the whole treasure thrown down the mountainside. The job fell to the 28th, as Cadell explains:

> The rear-guard, therefore, was halted; Lieutenant Bennet, of the light company, Twenty-eighth Regiment, was placed over the money, with strict orders from Sir John Moore to shoot the first person who attempted to touch it. It was then rolled over the precipice; the casks were soon broken by the rugged rocks, and the dollars falling out, rolled over the height – a sparkling cascade of silver.

This extraordinary sight did not have the desired effect, however. Whilst some of the coins that were deliberately scattered on the road did indeed hold up the French advance guard – who, not surprisingly, stopped to pick them up – it was noticed shortly afterwards that many of Moore's troops had started to lag behind. Slowly the men who had witnessed the cascade of silver were peeling off from the back of the column and returning to the coin-strewn hillside. That decision would not make any of their fortunes. Most of those who headed back, tempted by the loot, were captured by the French. Others who evaded capture froze to death in the icy mountain passes, trying to rejoin their column.

Accidents Will Happen

The chapter of knowledge is a very short one, but the chapter of accidents is a very long one.

Philip Dormer Stanhope, Earl of Chesterfield, letter to Solomon Dayrolles, 16 February 1753, in M. Maty (ed.), *Miscellaneous Works*, vol. 2 (1778), no. 79

What made Christian Schönbein's apron explode?

Among nineteenth-century chemists one of the most pressing, and potentially lucrative, areas of research was finding a replacement for gunpowder. Black powder had a number of drawbacks in that it left a dirty soot, clogging firearms. Furthermore, it exploded with a cloud of thick smoke that, in the case of a single soldier, gave away his location and, in the case of an army, could obscure an entire battlefield.

The race was on to find a replacement that would burn more cleanly and with less or preferably no smoke, but with at least the same energy as black powder. The winner could make a fortune. And nowhere was that race run with more enthusiasm, or more domestic tension, than in Christian Schönbein's household. Schönbein was a Swiss German chemist working in Basle, whose penchant for the more lively branches of chemistry had got him banned from conducting his research at home by his irate wife.

However, you can't keep a good chemist down and when Schönbein's wife was out he would secretly experiment in the kitchen. It was during just such a subterfuge in 1845 that he spilt some concentrated nitric acid on the table. Aware that this might give his little game away, he quickly grabbed the nearest cloth, which happened to be one of his wife's cotton aprons, and mopped it up, thoughtfully hanging it over the stove door to dry.

Schönbein was unaware that, in mopping up nitric acid with cotton, he had turned the cellulose in the apron into nitrocellulose, the properties of which were shortly demonstrated to him in no uncertain terms when the apron suddenly exploded. History does not record what Schönbein's wife said when she got home but the unexpected discovery would change the face of warfare. After much further experimenting, not in the kitchen this time, Schönbein perfected a method of making nitrocellulose with nitric acid, sulphuric acid and cotton wool, an explosive with six times the power of gunpowder but with much less heat and smoke generation, which was christened 'guncotton'.

In fact, nitrocellulose had been discovered before and by several chemists independently, although the use of cotton as the cellulose source was, entirely accidentally, all Schönbein's idea. Several governments soon began producing guncotton but in its raw form it proved as difficult to control as the original apron, blowing up several factories established to manufacture it. It would take many years of patient research by Frederick Abel, at the British government's Waltham Abbey Royal Gunpowder Mills, to tame the guncotton beast, making it safe and suitable as a replacement for gunpowder. Indeed, it would take another forty-six years before a fully stable form of guncotton would be developed. This could be shaped into long cords and was hence known as 'cordite'.

Why did Trooper Fowler live in a wardrobe?

Some soldiers spent the First World War on the front line, and some in prisoner-of-war camps, but Trooper Patrick Fowler of the 11th Hussars (Prince Albert's Own) spent his war in a cupboard or, more precisely, a small wardrobe.

The events leading up to Trooper Fowler's incarceration are extraordinary and his survival was not a little heroic. On 26 August 1914, Fowler found himself cut off from his regiment during the fighting at Le Cateau during a German advance. For nearly five months he survived alone in the local woods but he was discovered by a local man, Louis Basquin, in January 1915. Rather than hand over the weak and starving man to the Germans, Basquin took him to the house of his mother-in-law, Madame Belmont-Gobert, in the village of Bertry. Madame Belmont-Gobert and her daughter Angèle immediately agreed to hide the trooper in what was now German-occupied territory. No doubt all concerned believed this was a temporary solution until the Allies won back the village. However, this was not to be.

The German lines dug in well ahead of Madame Belmont-Gobert's farm and, to make matters worse, two weeks after the arrival of her unexpected guest she received more company when sixteen German soldiers were billeted in the house. It had been bad enough when Trooper Fowler had had to hide in the small wardrobe that Madame Belmont-Gobert had prepared for him at night to avoid patrols. The situation now became desperate as the Germans spent much of their time in the same room as the wardrobe, requiring Trooper Fowler to remain perfectly still and absolutely silent for hours on end. Only late at night could Madame Belmont-Gobert sneak her tommy out of his hiding place to stretch his legs and share the tiny amounts of food that the family had to live on.

Their predicament was relieved only by a near disaster. The German High Command sent orders that the whole farmhouse was to be requisitioned and its owner moved to a small cottage near by. With astonishing chutzpah, Madame Belmont-Gobert persuaded her German 'guests' to move her possessions to her new residence, including the wardrobe – with Fowler still inside it. Quite why no inquisitive German ever looked inside, or at least asked what exactly might be in such a weighty piece of furniture, remains a mystery. On the one occasion when the wardrobe was searched – during a hunt for concealed soldiers following the capture and execution of nurse Edith Cavell – Belmont-Gobert had hidden Fowler under the mattress instead, having, so she later claimed, had a premonition that the wardrobe would be searched.

In the new cottage Trooper Fowler had a little more freedom, but he still had to return to his wardrobe whenever the Germans approached as well as at night. Fowler's closeted existence continued until 10 October 1918 when the German forces finally evacuated Bertry. Fortunately for Fowler, the village was taken by his own regiment and so he managed to explain why he had been absent from the front for nearly four years without finding himself on a charge of desertion.

After the war Madame Belmont-Gobert, who would have been

shot together with Fowler if they had been discovered, was awarded the Order of the British Empire for her bravery, but in 1927 she was found to be living in dire poverty. Following a campaign led by the *Telegraph* newspaper to raise funds, she was eventually sent £100 by the 11th Hussars and then awarded full billeting pay by the British government for having cared for Patrick Fowler – back-dated to 1914. In response the French government also awarded her a pension. The cramped wardrobe, in which Patrick Fowler spent his war, now stands in the regimental museum in Winchester.

Why did the Italians sink a friendly dreadnought?

During the First World War the four big dreadnoughts of the Austrian fleet remained anchored in the Adriatic harbour of Pola but their inaction did not mean that the Italians, whose coasts their big guns still threatened, did not wish them at the bottom of the sea.

An occasion to achieve their wish finally arrived in 1918 with the invention of a daring underwater device known as the 'chariot'. This torpedo-shaped machine, thirty-three feet long, was designed to deliver two large mines to be placed on the hull of moored enemy ships and sink them.

The chariot was not an automatic device, however, merely a transporter, travelling three feet under the surface of the sea, powered by a compressed air motor, and being guided to its destination by two divers wearing rubber suits who rode atop it, their heads sticking out of the water. So it was that, on the night of 31 October, Major Raffaele Rossetti and Lieutenant Raffaele Paolucci, the best divers in the Italian navy, could be found in the gloom riding a chariot, skimming over anti-submarine nets and darting past scanning searchlights, into Pola harbour towards the huge Austrian battleship *Viribus Unitis*.

In poor weather conditions it was a feat of great skill and bravery simply to get alongside the *Viribus Unitis* but Rossetti and Paolucci managed it. After two hours of struggle, they positioned the mines on her hull and set the timers. By now there was not enough compressed air left in the chariot to return to the torpedo boat waiting for them out at sea so they decided to sink the machine and swim for it. It was at this point that they were spotted and captured.

To their horror the captured divers were now taken not ashore but on board the *Viribus Unitis*. As they knew it was due to explode just over an hour later, both men expected to die locked in her brig. So it was to their great surprise that, on boarding the ship, they were introduced, not to the Austrian, Admiral Horthy, but to the neutral Yugoslav, Captain Ianko Vukovic.

It was a big day for Captain Vukovic. The previous night the Austrian fleet, seeing which way the war was going, had mutinied and her admiral had handed over to him control of the *Viribus Unitis*. He now had his own dreadnought to command – but not for long. Rossetti immediately explained that the ship was in mortal danger but refused to explain exactly why, as it was still his intention to sink her, just not her neutral crew. Although taken aback, Vukovic gave the order to abandon ship and in the confusion Rossetti and Paolucci managed to jump overboard – only to be returned to the ship in a lifeboat by a group of angry sailors who, seeing them flee, assumed it was a hoax.

Back on board the two divers were again threatened by the understandably nervous crew who became more abusive when, at 6.30, the time the charges were due to detonate, nothing happened. Men who had abandoned ship now started to return until, fourteen minutes later, the mines finally detonated. As a huge column of water rose into the air and the ship began to list, Rossetti and Paolucci asked whether they might abandon ship. Captain Vukovic agreed and shook their hands, ushering them towards a rope leading down to the water. As the two men were rowed away in a lifeboat, they saw Captain Vukovic crawling up the upturned hull. It was the last time anyone saw him alive and he went down with his ship.

Rossetti and Paolucci were taken prisoner but released when

Italy and Austria signed an armistice three days later. Both men were given gold medals for courage and Rossetti received a 650,000 lire reward, which he, in turn, gave to Vukovic's widow. She used the money to establish a trust fund for the widows and mothers of war victims.

Who was the Grand Old Duke of York?

Every child knows of the Duke of York's apparently capricious orders to his men regarding marching up and down hills but the origins of the tale remain something of a mystery.

There are three main theories about just which Grand Old Duke is involved, what exactly his men are doing, and why. The first theory is that the rhyme dates from the Wars of the Roses when, late in 1460, Richard Plantagenet, 3rd Duke of York, took Sandal castle near Wakefield, only to find himself surrounded by a larger Lancastrian army. A wise duke might have stayed put but Richard, perhaps tricked by Edward Neville, 1st Baron Neville de Raby, riding under false colours, marched out from his strong point 'down the hill' to Wakefield Green where his army was decisively defeated and he was killed.

The second theory comes from a much later war and involved Prince Frederick Augustus, Duke of York and Albany, and the second son of King George III. Titles had always come easily to Frederick – he became Prince-Bishop of Osnabrück in Lower Saxony in 1764 when only 196 days old, making him the youngest bishop in history. His father made him a Knight of the Bath when he was four, a Knight of the Garter when he was eight and Duke of York and Albany at twenty-one. Perhaps not surprisingly, he was also a field marshal and commander-in-chief of the British army – titles he received not as a reward for years of experience but at the end of one campaign in Flanders in 1793.

His first command as C-in-C was the invasion of Holland, an operation undertaken jointly with the Russians, which began well but ended in a humiliating withdrawal, due at least in part to the duke's understandable inexperience. The campaign culminated in the town of Castricum changing hands several times, between the French and Dutch on one side and the British and Russians on the other, until the latter finally fled in a chaotic retreat in which they 'forgot' two of their field hospitals, leaving them and their inmates behind in the confusion. This defeat may have given rise to the rhyme as a way of ridiculing the duke's decision-making although, at the age of only thirty-one, he might be forgiven for lacking experience. In time he would actually make up for this embarrassment, using his position to insist that men rose through the ranks, not, as he had done, by preferment, but strictly on merit. He also founded Sandhurst to ensure that the field marshals who followed him would have the necessary training to do the job and not just the father to give it to them.

The final theory also involves Frederick but in a more kindly, if rather eccentric, role and has no military connotations at all. Frederick bought Allerton castle in 1786 and decided to build a 'temple of victory' on a two-hundred-foot hill in the grounds, as was the fashion of the day. The sight of the workers labouring up and down this hill to build the duke's folly is said by some to be the origin of the rhyme.

Other theories also exist, including one that the Grand Old Duke was James II, formerly Duke of York and the man after whom New York was named, who was remembered in rhyme for his refusal to fight William of Orange during the Glorious Revolution. Still older versions have different leaders leading their men up hill and down dale. It is likely that there never really was one single prototype, and that rhymes like this have been used for centuries to tease any military leader who can't make up his mind.

What was the fastest retreat in history?

There is a time to fight and a time, frankly, to run away but in making a 'tactical withdrawal' it is always advisable to keep a sense of proportion.

Charge!

During the Irish rebellion of 1798 against British rule, the French, keen to cause a bit of trouble for the British, sent the French general, Jean Joseph Amable Humbert, and his army to support the rebels. They had intended and were expected to land in Donegal but due to adverse weather ended up near Killala in southern Ireland. Not only was he in the wrong place but, unbeknown to Humbert, the larger French force commanded by General Jean Hardy, which he was meant to join up with, had never left France because of unfavourable winds. Nevertheless he set about recruiting local Irishmen and preparing for battle.

This confusion seemed to present a great opportunity for the British general Cornwallis when he heard of the landings and he quickly got together a force of soldiers from various garrisons to take on the Franco-Irish army. On 27 August the two armies met just outside Castlebar in County Mayo.

Initially the battle favoured Cornwallis as his artillery cut into the enemy ranks but the French, rather to his surprise, countered with a ferocious bayonet charge. So fierce did this prove that the British began to waver, some deciding that now would be a good moment to announce their new-found desire to join the rebels, whilst the majority decided simply to run. Just how impressive this French counter-attack must have been can be judged from their running. Leaving equipment and artillery behind, abandoning their general's personal baggage train, they ran in some cases as far as Athlone in a single day. When you consider that Athlone is sixty-three miles away, this becomes perhaps the fastest, non-mechanised retreat in military history. What makes it even more surprising is that the French gave up pursuit after just two miles but Cornwallis's cross-country runners didn't stop for another sixty-one. Had not Cornwallis himself arrived at Athlone, it was said that many might have run even further.

This humiliation was short-lived – the French quickly surrendering when they found themselves outnumbered twenty to one by Cornwallis's main army – but it remains one of the least illustrious and least talked about moments in British military history.

The rebels certainly did talk about it, however, the event becoming known in Irish history as 'the Castlebar Races'.

How did General de Ros escape the Crimean War?

General William Lennox Lascelles FitzGerald de Ros, 23rd Baron de Ros, was a third son and as such was always intended for a military career, but his invaliding out of the Crimean War must be one of the most unusual such circumstance in British military history.

De Ros had joined the Life Guards in 1819 and risen through the ranks until in 1854 he was appointed quartermaster general – the staff officer in charge of supplies for the whole army. That particular year was a busy time for any quartermaster as the Crimean War had officially begun on 28 March. The following month de Ros was posted to Varna on the Bulgarian coast of the Black Sea to prepare the way for the British army expedition.

By all accounts de Ros, with thirty-five years' experience in the army, was a great success and it was reported that he worked at his assignment 'like a slave', although this did not prevent him from indulging his little idiosyncrasies. Whilst it is well known that mad dogs and Englishmen go out in the midday sun, most of the men at Varna took the precaution of staying out of the hot Bulgarian sun as much as possible. All except Baron de Ros. A first-hand, anonymous account by a staff officer of the preparations for war, published by John Murray in 1856, noted of de Ros: 'he is certainly very eccentric, both in his habits and dress; very amusing, too. One of his fancies is to go out as much as possible in the sun! which he insists on doing, although warned by the medical men that there is great danger attending it.'

This predilection would prove his undoing. De Ros is one of the first recorded sun worshippers in British history and certainly the first in the army. His habit of sunbathing in hot climes led to sunstroke and he was invalided back to Britain, just before the British army, which he had prepared for so enthusiastically, embarked for the Crimea, making him the first high-ranking casualty of the war, before battle had even been joined.

Why did Napoleon's generals shoot at each other?

It is not always left to the enemy to kill the leading officers of an army. Sometimes armies manage to get rid of their commanders without any outside help whatsoever.

General Jacques-Zacharie Destaing had made an illustrious career for himself in Napoleon's army. He had fought bravely in the Army of Italy, receiving several sabre wounds, and had so impressed Napoleon at the Battle of the Pyramids, during the Egyptian campaign, that he had promoted him to *général de brigade* on the spot. More battle honours and more wounds followed, until Destaing rose to become chief of staff in Egypt under the command of General Menou.

At the same time, General Jean-Louis-Ebénézer Reynier was also cutting a dash. Reynier had first joined the army as a volunteer gunner during the revolution and his rise had been meteoric. At just twenty-three years of age he had turned down a promotion to general on the grounds that he was too young for the job. The following year he was asked again and this time accepted. Hence he too found his way into Napoleon's Egyptian campaign as one of his most trusted officers.

It was in Egypt, however, that these two potential French heroes fatally clashed. Reynier was openly hostile to Menou's command, somewhat piquing the general who ordered his chief of staff, Destaing, to arrest his troublesome comrade for treason. Having little choice, Destaing complied, although Reynier was later absolved of any crime.

But Reynier would not let the matter rest there. Back in Paris later that year he published a letter attacking Menou and his staff and began suggesting that Destaing, who had arrested him, had made a rather cowardly withdrawal from the Battle of Alexandria when only slightly wounded. This was a red rag to a bull. Both generals now felt that their honour was impugned, so when Destaing demanded satisfaction for the slur, Reynier readily agreed.

On 5 May 1802 the two great generals met with pistols to fight a duel to the death. Moments later General Jacques-Zacharie Destaing received a pistol shot to the chest and promptly expired, leaving France's enemies with one less heroic general to defeat, courtesy of another. Napoleon was furious and banished Reynier – at least until he needed him again.

Who was the last casualty of the Battle of Blenheim?

A very good time to find out exactly what your men think of you is on the battlefield. With enemy guns pointing at you from the front and 'friendly' guns from the rear, a hated commander can soon find out just how unpopular he really is. Of course in the heat of battle it can be very difficult to discover who exactly fired a fatal shot and, no doubt, many a score between supposed allies has been settled in the fog of combat in this way.

One such story, albeit with an unnamed commander, was widely reported to have taken place on the day of the Battle of Blenheim, in the War of the Spanish Succession. As the British troops under Marlborough were mustering for the battle, a major in the 15th Foot decided to address his soldiers. A thoroughly unpleasant and widely disliked commander, he knew that his men had no love for him and, realising that perhaps his hour had come, he decided to take a frank view of what might lie ahead. Apologising to them for his former bad behaviour, he begged them that, if he should fall in battle, it should at least be to one of the enemy's bullets and not one of his own men's. If, however, he survived the battle he promised to try much harder in future to be a decent chap.

A grovelling apology probably isn't what his soldiers were expecting just at that point but, whatever they thought in their hearts, with the fighting about to commence they promised that they would be far too busy to attack their own major, making it safe for him to lead them onto the field (or safe from his own troops, at least).

The regiment performed well and, after several attempts, they had carried the position they had been ordered to take. Delighted that the fortunes of war were with them and that he was still alive, the major turned to his men, raised his hat and shouted, 'Gentlemen, the day is ours.' At this moment a bullet hit him four-square in the forehead and he dropped to the ground dead. The day might belong to his men but they were clearly determined that it wasn't going to belong to him. Needless to say, it was never discovered where the mysterious stray bullet came from.

What were the Germans doing in Suffolk in 1943?

As the Second World War progressed, the battle in the air grew ever more dominated by electronic warfare as the Axis and Allied forces tried to guide their own aircraft safely to their targets and back home again, whilst evading the electronic listening and jamming devices of the enemy. It was a high-tech war fought with the very latest equipment but that could all count for nothing when human error entered the equation.

By mid-1943 what particularly worried the British was the fact that their jamming procedures used against airborne radar – employed by German fighters to home in on British bombers – was proving less than successful, indicating that the Germans had introduced a new and improved system. Without being able to examine a sample, Bomber Command was particularly vulnerable.

Then as luck would have it an extraordinary event took place. On the night of 13 July 1944 a pilot officer at RAF Woodbridge in Suffolk noticed a plane circling overhead. As Woodbridge was one of the three RAF bases designed specifically to receive bombers that were badly damaged or low on fuel, he assumed the plane to be in trouble and sent up a flare to guide it in. The plane duly arced round and landed on the runway. It was only as the ground party went over to meet the crew, now that the aircraft was at a standstill, that both guests and reception committee had something of a shock. The plane was not the British Mosquito they had taken it to be but a German Ju88 G-1 night fighter, which had been on patrol over the North Sea. The ground crew produced a pistol, the crew wisely surrendered and the technical boys were called in to look at the pristine technological wonder now gracing Woodbridge's runway.

And they were not disappointed. The Ju88 was fitted with the very latest German technology including the FuG 220 Lichtenstein SN-2 radar, whose frequency had previously baffled the British. For good measure it was also carrying a FuG 2287 Flensburg passive radar, which could home in on the Monica tail-warning radar fitted to British bombers. As a result the Monica radars were removed from all British bombers and a device known as 'Window' (pieces of aluminium foil dropped from planes to confuse radar, now called 'chaff') was made to the right length to fool the Lichtenstein radar.

So how had all this fallen into British hands so easily? The answer was desperately human. The Ju88 crew, with only 100 hours' training under their belts, had flown on exactly the opposite bearing to the one they thought they were on. At the time the flare went up they believed they were over their own German airfield and so handed the pride of German technology to the British on a plate.

Unlikely Armour

To endeavour, all one's days, to fortify our minds with learning and philosophy, is to spend so much in armour that one has nothing left to defend.

William Shenstone, *Works* . . . (1764), vol. 2, 'On Writing and Books'

What was the most revolutionary ship ever built?

From the first prehistoric dugouts to the latest nuclear aircraft carriers, there have been many ship designs over the centuries but most conform to the basic plan of being longer than they are wide. This, after all, makes a vessel stable and easier to steer through water, something every good ship should be able to do.

But wasn't this just dogma? That at least is what Russian vice admiral A.A. Popov thought. After all, a ship that was round would have less of a surface area needing armour plate and hence could be either faster or more heavily protected, as well as being more manoeuvrable and at the same time more stable. This seemed to be just what Russia, which had recently lost a war against France and Britain, needed to protect the ports and river mouths of the Black Sea.

So in 1873, work began in the Russian dockyards on the first of two circular, flat-bottomed ironclads. The ships, which were completely circular when viewed from the air, were driven by six engines, each powering one propeller, whilst the firepower came from a pair of eleven-inch, rifled, breech-loading guns. The first such monstrous vessel was the 2,490-ton *Novgorod*. Three years later the *Kiev* was laid down at Nicolaiev, although her name was soon changed to the *Rear-Admiral Popov* in honour of its far-sighted originator.

What followed probably explains why you rarely see circular ships today. For all the theory, in practice these 'popovkas', as they were affectionately known, were ridiculous. Their bulbous shape meant that even with six engines they were capable of only around 6–7 knots, less than the current on the Dnieper river where they were tested and where they were promptly swept out to sea. Being not only round but flat-bottomed, they were also remarkably difficult to keep steady and as they were borne away they span round repeatedly, making the crew sick. Then there was the problem with the guns. As the ships were round and the guns were not exactly central, when they were fired they made the whole ship rotate. This meant that the guns and gunners were no longer facing in the direction they were firing in, although they made for a very amusing revolving target.

Needless to say, the popovkas were never deployed in an open sea battle, although to be fair that was never intended to be their role. Indeed, as no one could really work out just what their role was, they ended their days as storeships on permanent anchorages – much to the relief of their crews.

How did red trousers undo the French?

Over the centuries the nature of warfare has changed dramatically and with it the appearance of the soldiers who fight it. During the Napoleonic wars, when battles were often fought with tens of thousands of men on open fields, brightly coloured uniforms helped commanders to identify their men and their dispositions, as well as boosting the morale of the troops. Some regimental commanders spent thousands of pounds of their own money ensuring that their unit was the proudest and best dressed in the army. This was a time when the uniform really did make the man.

By the beginning of the twentieth century, however, warfare had changed, open set-piece battles were largely a thing of the past, and the increasing range of rifles meant it was generally best to keep your head down. The British therefore began putting aside their colourful uniforms after the Boer War and introduced khaki, whilst the Germans turned from Prussian blue to field grey in 1910. Most countries realised that this drab future was a necessity – most countries, that is, except France.

The French uniform in the run-up to the First World War had changed little since the days of the Second Empire, consisting in its most basic form of bright-red trousers, blue jacket, a dark-blue greatcoat and a kepi. As a uniform it was a source of great pride among the commanders of the French army, in particular the red trousers, which had been introduced in 1829 in an attempt to boost the French dye industry. For Adolphe Méssimy, French minister for war during the Balkan Wars of 1912–13, however, it seemed something of an anachronism. With the rest of the armies of the world dressing in dull tones, Méssimy, in 1912, suggested quite reasonably that perhaps the French uniform should change too.

The response must have come as something of a surprise. There were howls of protest from the army and the French press openly ridiculed the man who would do away with her soldiers' red trousers. The *rapporteur* of the war budget commented that 'To banish all that is colourful, all that gives the soldier his gay and spirited appearance . . . is to go against French tastes and military need.' Other politicians joined the fray, Alphonse Etienne announcing in stirring terms that 'Le Pantalon rouge, c'est la France,' whilst one of his compatriots chipped in, 'It is a legendary uniform.'

Legendary it might be, but practical it was not, although, tragically, the French establishment had to be given a bloody demonstration of the error of their ways. At the outbreak of war, during the First Battle of the Marne, the French went in to fight in their blue jackets and bright-red trousers. One regiment, marching through fields yellow with corn, could not have made for a clearer or easier target and the Germans cut them down from well over a kilometre away. Almost none of them survived.

Finally even the French politicians realised that the days of *le pantalon rouge* were gone. From April 1915, soft hats were replaced with steel helmets and the brilliant uniforms made way for the drab of 'bleu clair'.

Adolphe Méssimy would later write, ruefully: 'That blind and imbecilic attachment to the most visible of all colours was to have cruel consequences.'

What made William the Bastard so sensitive?

Military commanders can be touchy creatures when it comes to personal insults and none was more so than William, Duke of

Normandy. William was the son of Robert I of Normandy and had inherited the dukedom from his dad at the tender age of seven. Ruling his lands was no mean feat in the eleventh century and the young William soon learnt to fight for what was his, defending his land and titles against all forms of impostors, pretenders, counter-claimants and good old-fashioned invaders.

He proved remarkably good at this, so good in fact that he managed to take over a whole new kingdom – England – turning himself in the process from Duke William into King William. But William had another name, one that might have toppled a lesser man from his exalted position. William's father was undoubtedly Robert I but his mother was certainly not Robert's wife. The fact that William was the illegitimate son of Robert and his mistress Herleva was something of an open secret. Whilst Dad was known as 'Robert the Magnificent' (or 'Robert the Devil' to those who suspected him of murdering his own brother to get the dukedom), his son was known as 'William the Bastard'.

This nickname was not perhaps quite as bad as it sounds, coming from an age when illegitimacy was not necessarily an impediment to power – provided you were strong enough to defeat anyone who might claim it was. Nor was this an era when nicknames were unusual. Whilst any right-minded prince would obviously prefer something like 'the Magnificent', Ralph Tesson, for example, put up with being known as 'Ralph the Badger'.

However, it never pays to rub an angry duke's nose in the fact of his illegitimacy, as the burghers of Alençon would find out. In the autumn and winter of 1048–9, William was fighting in support of King Henry I of France against the rebellious count of Anjou and Maine, which involved besieging the city of Alençon. Its inhabitants were well aware of William's ancestry and, forgetting his military reputation, recklessly teased him about it. As William's mother, Herleva, was reputed to be the daughter of a common tanner called Fulbert, the burghers of the city hung animal hides from the walls and windows, and shouted, 'Hides for the tanner,' at William.

Being called a bastard was one thing but being called the son of a tanner was beyond the pale. William swore that when he took the city he would round up those who had mocked him and cut off their hands with a tree-pollarding knife.

Sure enough, the town did fall and William had the hands of thirty-two burghers cut off as he had sworn. As the castle in Alençon was still holding out, he had these limbs tossed over the wall, which had the desired effect of getting the garrison to surrender. Indeed, so shocked were people by William's ruthless behaviour that the nearby city of Domfront, keen to keep its burghers intact, surrendered too.

Seventeen years later William's formidable reputation was confirmed when he stood triumphant on the battlefield at Hastings, an act for which he would be known ever after not as 'the bastard' but as 'the conqueror'.

What innovation created the Fokker scourge?

Despite its being the era of the birth of aviation, the air commanders of the First World War proved wonderfully resistant to any new technology that might offer their pilots the edge in battle. The most astonishing example was their entire indifference to 'interruptor gear' – or, more correctly, 'synchronisation gear'.

Fighting in the air required that pilots or their crew fire guns at their opposite numbers. This was agreed upon by all involved. The question at the beginning of the war was how best to do this in fragile planes made of canvas and wood, powered by a vulnerable wooden propeller. Obviously the best configuration for a pilot would be to have the guns right in front of him so that he could look down the barrel and fire in his direction of travel, but this presented one apparently insurmountable problem – the propeller. In most aircraft this was also directly in front of the pilot and firing through it would quickly reduce it, and hence the plane, to matchwood.

What was needed was either a propeller that could deflect bullets or a mechanism that ensured the machine-guns fired a bullet only when the propeller blades were clear of the line of fire. If this could be achieved, the fighter plane would in effect become a flying gun, its pilot able to hit whatever was in front of him. Needless to say, the High Command thought this wholly unnecessary.

French pilot Roland Garros – after whom the French national tennis stadium is named, and one of the greatest airmen of his day – did think it was necessary and he became the first pilot of the war to use a forward-firing, 'through-the-prop' gun. Between 1 and 18 April 1915, Garros shot down three planes.

Then, on one sortie, a clogged fuel line forced him to ditch behind enemy lines. Having landed his plane safely, Garros became acutely aware that his forward-firing system was likely to fall into enemy hands so he desperately tried to set fire to his aircraft. Unfortunately this rather unusual behaviour had exactly the wrong effect, alerting the Germans to the possibility that this otherwise ordinary machine was in fact something special. The plane was seized and sent for evaluation. The advantage of forward-firing guns was immediately clear to the Germans and, with the help of Dutch designer Anthony Fokker, they developed an enhanced synchronisation system, leading to a period of German air superiority known as the 'Fokker scourge'.

It was only in April 1916, when a batch of Fokker aircraft fitted with the gear accidentally landed at a British aerodrome, rather than the German one they were meant to be heading for, that the British finally got their hands on the synchronisation gear and decided to give it a go themselves. The era of the Fokker scourge finally came to an end.

How did Daphne du Maurier expose a spy ring?

The story of how Daphne du Maurier helped break a Nazi spy ring in Egypt is one of the more remarkable tales of the Second

World War and it owes its origins to the literary tastes of the wife of a German military attaché in Portugal.

The German Kondor mission of 1942 was designed to place two spies, John Eppler and Peter Monkaster, in British-controlled Cairo to gather intelligence for Rommel's North African campaign. Initially the scheme achieved its objective. The two men infiltrated the city and took a houseboat on the Nile, secreting one radio transmitter in the bilges and another behind the altar of a local church run by a pro-German Austrian priest.

Eppler was also fortunate to run into Hekmeth Fahmy, an Arab nationalist belly dancer who just happened to be having an affair with a 'Major Smith' of the headquarters staff of the British army in Cairo. Having satisfied each other of their anti-British credentials, she agreed to let Eppler search and photograph the contents of Major Smith's attaché case while she and the major were making love.

With hard intelligence now reaching Rommel, Operation Kondor looked like a complete success, so Eppler and Monkaster extended their remit to attempting to inspire an Arab jihad against the Allies. But a series of crucial mistakes would soon bring the whole plan tumbling down.

Eppler, who had been in Cairo before the war, went to the Turf Club, dressed as a British officer, to gather the gossip. He decided to pay for his drink with one of the 50,000 fake British pound notes that he had been given by the Germans. Eppler knew that British money was accepted but he didn't know that it now had to be handed in to the British paymaster for conversion into local currency.

Later that same evening he made another mistake, picking up a bar girl called Yvette, whom he took for a local prostitute, and taking her back to his houseboat. Yvette was actually working for the Jewish Agency, which reported the two men to MI6. She told her handlers that Eppler had a German Saarland accent, was very nervous and had far too much money – in other words, he was a spy.

Three days later Yvette returned to the houseboat and, while Eppler and Monkaster slept, searched the vessel. In the main lounge she came across a book and, near by, a page of gridded squares with groups of six letters in it, which were clearly used for coding. Allowing the book to fall open onto the most-read pages, she noted down both the grid and the page numbers before making her escape. As she left she was arrested by an MI6 agent, who was watching the boat but who had not been told about her, and taken into custody.

Meanwhile MI6 had a bigger problem on their hands. They had recently captured a German wireless intelligence unit but were somewhat baffled by what they found on them – a copy of Daphne du Maurier's *Rebecca* in English. *Mein Kampf* was a common discovery but the works of du Maurier were a shade unusual among front-line German troops, which made them suspicious. A further examination of the book showed it had been bought in Portugal. The bookshop in Estoril was soon located, and confirmed that the wife of a German military attaché had purchased six copies the previous April. Clearly *Rebecca* was being used as a cipher but who was using it?

At this point Eppler's first mistake came back to haunt him. The British paymaster had noticed the new British pound notes coming to his office and had identified them as German fakes, which had been linked back to the 'British officer' at the Turf Club. He was then traced to the houseboat. In the ensuing raid both Eppler and Monkaster were taken but Monkaster managed to dump most of their equipment through the bilges beforehand. With neither man prepared to talk, and no codebook or radio, the British were stymied. Fahmy the belly dancer did talk, however, and the source of their information – Major Smith – was finally silenced. Some days later the British had another stroke of luck when the houseboat was raised (it had sunk when the bilges were opened). Underneath it was found the radio, unusable but still set to the last transmission frequency. If the British could now work out the code they were using, they could send false intelligence to Rommel.

But Eppler still refused to talk, even after an elaborate mock court martial left him waiting for the firing squad. By this time the Jewish Agency had finally spoken to MI6 about Yvette and obtained her release. She mentioned to the discharging officer that she had been on Eppler's houseboat. He asked her whether she had seen a book lying around when she was there. Of course, she replied – it was a copy of Daphne du Maurier's *Rebecca*. Thinking it odd, she had copied down the gridded squares that she'd found next to it and noted the most-thumbed pages of the novel. These notes were immediately sent on to MI6 and from them the *Rebecca* code was cracked. Within a week Operation Kondor was back in business, as far as the Germans were concerned, and a constant flow of misleading information was fed to Rommel that would alter the course of the war in North Africa.

What was the first stealth bomber?

One of the main snags with bomber aircraft is that they tend to be large and slow, making them easy targets, a fact not lost on even the earliest aeroplane designers. Ever since a pilot and crew first clambered aboard one of these hulking, sluggish machines, they have wished that they might be invisible and fly unseen over enemy territory. In 1916 the German aircraft manufacturer Linke-Hoffman of Breslau decided to try to make that dream come true.

In that year the German government awarded Linke-Hoffman the contract to build one of their 'R-planes' – the 'R' standing for *Riesenflugzeug* or 'giant aircraft'. To be honest, a first attempt at stealth technology should probably have been attempted on something a shade smaller than the R-planes, which were the largest flying machines of the whole war, but Linke-Hoffman were undeterred.

The plane that they built was over fifteen and a half metres long with a wingspan of over thirty-three metres, propelled by four 260-horsepower Mercedes engines and known as the 'R1'. It was never going to be easy to make this monstrous aircraft disappear but the company believed they had a secret weapon. Instead of covering the fuselage behind the cockpit with doped canvas, they intended to use a high-tech material called Cellon, which was transparent and would therefore, they thought, make at least half the plane invisible.

There were three main problems with this innovative stealth technology. First, Cellon, a type of cellulose, was hugely inflammable, although it could be argued that all aircraft at that date were tinderboxes. Second, it wasn't very strong or stable, meaning that in dry weather the material shrank, warping the fuselage, whilst in damp weather it expanded, making the whole structure sag. It also decayed in ultraviolet light, yellowing, becoming brittle, and occasionally explosively shattering. But it was the third drawback that really sealed the machine's fate. Cellon was transparent but very shiny, meaning that in flight the plane almost glowed as the sunlight bounced off its shimmering sides. It would be difficult at that date to have found a more obvious object in the sky.

The R1 only ever made two flights. On the first, the wheels fell off and, when the plane finally got airborne, the pilot, sitting in his sweltering Cellon cockpit, found the controls so soft that he couldn't steer. On the second flight, in May 1917, the wings fell off and the plane hit the ground vertically. Amazingly the pilot survived. After this the R1 project was shelved.

Who went into battle with a spare leg?

Lieutenant General Richard Stoddart Ewell was one of the corps commanders of Confederate general Robert E. Lee and one of the luckiest men at the Battle of Gettysburg.

Ewell came from an old military family and had been trained at the West Point military academy. He was popular with his men, who rather brazenly called him 'Old Bald Head' or 'Baldy', but he suffered from debilitating illnesses following an injury he received fighting the Apaches in 1859.

Following the outbreak of the American Civil War and the

secession of his home state of Virginia from the Union, he had resigned his commission in the US army to join the Confederates. His part in Thomas 'Stonewall' Jackson's Shenandoah Valley campaign proved a great success, the two men's eccentric but differing styles of command working brilliantly together. It was during this period that, paradoxically, a potentially life-saving injury befell him. At the Second Battle of Bull Run, he received a musket shot to the right leg, which shattered the bone and led to the limb having to be amputated. Having been nursed back to health by his future wife, he rejoined the Army of Northern Virginia.

Ewell returned to the fray, sporting a fine new wooden leg, just in time for promotion as his old mentor, Jackson, had been accidentally shot by his own troops after the Battle of Chancellorsville and later died from complications. General Lee now placed him, as Jackson had suggested on his deathbed, in charge of 2nd Corps for the beginning of the Gettysburg campaign.

Almost from the start Ewell proved personally lucky, being shot in the chest at the Second Battle of Winchester, but by a spent ball that simply glanced off. It was the second time that that had happened to him in the war, the first being at Gaines's Mill on 27 July 1862. At the Battle of Gettysburg he proved yet more fortunate. While reconnoitring the town, he was warned that as Union sharpshooters were lying in wait on Cemetery Hill, he should not advance further. Perhaps now feeling invulnerable, he laughed off the warning, saying that the snipers were a full 1,500 yards distant and could never hit him from there. He was then reminded that he had already had one horse shot out from beneath him two days earlier, so perhaps it was best not to tempt fate, advice that he similarly ignored. Twenty paces further down the street Captain Richardson, riding next to him, was shot in the chest and moments later the rest of the party heard the news they all dreaded when Ewell himself announced that he'd also been hit.

General John B. Gordon, who was with Ewell, recorded later that he heard the thud of the ball striking his commanding officer and turned to ask, 'Are you hurt, sir?' Astonishingly, Ewell grinned back and announced: 'I'm not hurt. But suppose that ball had struck you: we would have had the trouble of carrying you off the field, sir. You see how much better fixed for a fight I am than you are. It don't hurt a bit to be shot in a wooden leg.' He then sent for his spare leg, which he fitted on before riding away.

Although Ewell was seemingly invulnerable, the rest of the battle did not go well for him. He was accused of failing to take Cemetery Hill and of lacking the initiative needed to command a corps. Lee eventually relieved Ewell of his command and appointed him instead to head the garrison of Richmond until he was captured at the Battle of Sayler's Creek. Soon afterwards, Lee surrendered and Ewell managed to live out the rest of his life in peace as a farmer.

Why shouldn't you give a pilot a parachute?

The most valuable commodity in warfare is surely the highly trained soldier himself. Armour, machinery, buildings and supplies can be found, replaced, patched up and repaired – but the human being on the front line is priceless. This was very much not the view of the British Royal Flying Corps in the First World War.

Flying at that time was a dangerous business and not just because of the enemy; indeed, over half the British pilot fatalities (more than 8,000) occurred in training. The problem for a pilot was very simple: when an aeroplane goes wrong in flight, you can't simply pull into a layby, pop the bonnet up and try and tinker with the engine. Traditionally you plummet downwards as fast as gravity will permit, a process that tends to spoil both plane and pilot on landing.

But was it necessary to condemn every pilot whose plane was shot down or broke down to such an inevitable death? Not really, as there was a perfectly adequate escape mechanism – the parachute. The drawback was that the British High Command didn't like its men using them. The parachute had been invented by the

Frenchman, André Jacques Garnerin, who made the first successful jump in 1797 from a balloon, and parachutes were usually issued to balloon spotters in the First World War. However, they were not issued to British pilots.

The reasons given were many, some likely, but many spurious. Certainly there was a feeling among the more macho elements of the flying establishment that parachutes were a bit 'effete'. *Flight* magazine claimed, in 1913: 'A pilot's job is to stick to his aeroplane.' This peculiar idea, that falling to certain death was somehow 'manly', infiltrated the Royal Flying Corps, which came up with numerous reasons why parachutes couldn't be issued, claiming they were too bulky, too unreliable, too heavy, and would be no use when most accidents happened, which was at take-off and landing.

What is clear from the discussion that the High Command had when given parachutes to test – in 1915 – is that the real reason they wouldn't issue them was that they encouraged cowardliness and a reckless attitude towards government property. In other words, the prevailing view of the commanders was that, given half a chance, any pilot would run away, bail out and wreck his plane, unless he had no option but to stay in it and fight. It was pointed out that having a parachute might make pilots more eager to engage in battle as they stood more chance of surviving, but these protests were ignored.

When E.R. Calthrop, the British inventor of the 1915 parachute, who had patented one that he called the 'Guardian Angel', ignored RFC instructions and started selling his parachutes privately to British pilots, the Air Board was forced to look at the question again. It concluded: 'It is the opinion of the board that the presence of such an apparatus might impair the fighting spirit of pilots and cause them to abandon machines which might otherwise be capable of returning to base for repair.'

As a result the issuing of parachutes to pilots was refused, despite the fact that US, French and German pilots were now using them; indeed, one of Germany's greatest aces, Ernst Udet, was saved by one. Calthrop was dismissed by the British but the Russians bought 100 of his devices. One of these fell into German hands and was copied, ensuring that at least German pilots benefited from Calthrop's invention.

How did cheap tea start a war?

It's not often that a war starts over something being too cheap but, contrary to popular opinion, that is exactly what lit the fuse on the American Revolutionary War.

As the tale is normally told, on 16 December 1773 around fifty American patriots dressed as Mohawk Indians went down to Boston harbour where the British East Indiamen *Eleanor*, *Dartmouth* and *Beaver* were alongside at Griffin wharf. Climbing aboard, they took the 90,000-pound cargo of British tea and dumped it in the harbour. Nothing else was attacked or broken, save for one padlock, which was later anonymously replaced.

But this protest was not all that it seemed. The men busy turning Boston harbour into the world's largest cup of tea were not complaining that the cargo was too expensive, due to British taxes, but that it was too cheap. American colonies had been buying their tea from non-British merchants and hence avoiding the tax payable to the British government. In response, the British government had given the East India Company what was in effect a monopoly. This allowed the East Indiamen to trade direct with the colonies and not via Britain, which actually made East India tea cheaper than that sold by local merchants. To make matters worse from the point of view of the Bostonians the British government also reduced the tax burden on the East India Company. It was this that really infuriated some of the burghers of Boston.

The British government wasn't going to take this lying down, of course, and so in 1774 parliament passed what the colonists called 'the Intolerable Acts', which punished the colonies for insubordination. One of these was the Boston Port Bill, which shut the port to all trade until the Bostonians had paid for the tea they had destroyed.

Helped by British heavy-handedness, the nature of the Bostonians' gripe was by now transmogrifying from a protest over the price of tea to something deeper. Why, leaders such as Samuel Adams asked, should colonists pay any tax to the British government when they had no representation in parliament? And so what had started as a dispute over cheap tea imports turned into the *casus belli* for war and independence.

The Great Game

The great fallacy is that the game is first and last about winning. It is nothing of the kind. The game is about glory, it is about doing things in style and with a flourish, about going out and beating the lot, not waiting for them to die of boredom.

Danny Blanchflower, *Oxford Dictionary of Quotations* (attrib. 1972)

Where was the safest place at the Battle of Waterloo?

Because of the epic scale of the Battle of Waterloo, we often forget that it was fought on ordinary land, with outbuildings, barns and farmhouses, not simply on a vast empty plain. In fact, some of the most dangerous action took place in unlikely surroundings.

One such place was the farm of La Haye Sainte, which lieutenants Graeme and Carey and Ensign Frank of the King's German Legion were defending. The struggle was bitter and by 6 p.m., after a day of almost continuous fighting, they were without ammunition. Another attack, this time led in person by Napoleon's commander Marshal Ney, sent the German Legion reeling back, under devastating fire from the other side of the garden hedge. In the house the situation now became desperate as the attackers made a final push to seize it. By now the French were already in the downstairs passage and, seeing an enemy soldier levelling his weapon, Frank shouted to Lieutenant Graeme to take care. Graeme, with all the pluck of a *Boy's Own* hero, replied, 'Never mind. Let the rascal fire!' It might have been the last thing Lieutenant Graeme ever said, had not Frank taken the precaution of stabbing the owner of the gun before he got a chance to loose off a round.

At this point their plight went from bad to worse as the French began pouring into the house. Lieutenant Graeme was surrounded by the enemy who had the temerity to call him a 'coquin' (or mischief maker). The insult gave Graeme the time he needed to draw his sword, parry their bayonet thrusts and make good his escape. Matters were not so simple for Frank. In protecting his friend, his right arm had been shattered by a French bullet, and now his escape route was cut off. The only thing to do was go upstairs and hide in the bedroom.

Frank and two others dashed upstairs, closely followed by the enemy. In the bedroom the French confronted Frank's two compatriots with the cry, 'Pas de pardon à ces coquins verds' – making absolutely clear their opinion of those who run away. They then promptly shot them dead. This, however, gave Frank time to hide under the bed, where he managed to remain undiscovered, the enemy believing apparently that they had cleared the building of *coquins*. From here he listened, so the propaganda sheets tell us, to the comings and goings of the French troops, the murder of British prisoners and a lot of thoroughly bad language, all the time entirely unable to move, let alone escape.

Fortunately, outside the bed, the room and the house, the tide of battle was turning and the arrival of the Prussians under Generalfeldmarschall Blücher sent the French into retreat. Sometime just before 9 p.m. La Haye Sainte was recaptured and Ensign Frank could emerge from under the bed to tell his extraordinary tale.

What got Broughall in a pickle?

It used to be said that if you wanted to get ahead, you needed to get a hat, and Broughall, a Canadian with the 9th Royal Sussex regiment on the Somme on 7 July 1916, seemed particularly keen to get both. To be fair, hats can be quite important in trench warfare, particularly the metal variety, which had been introduced by the British earlier that year. As might be expected, the direct consequence was a 75 per cent reduction in head wounds. In spite of this, not all commanders immediately approved their introduction, fearing that replacing soft foraging caps with steel helmets might make their men go soft (see page 234 for a similarly hard-hearted attitude towards parachutes for airmen).

The German forces offered a whole new experience in hats – as far as the British were concerned, of course. Although the steel helmet was starting to become standard issue for the German army too, many soldiers could still be found sporting a Pickelhaube – the polished-leather Prussian helmet with a decorative metal spike on the top. This proved that the German High Command had been just as indifferent to the welfare of their men as had the Allies, since the Pickelhaube not only offered almost no protection from shell fragments, but the spike poking up over the rim of the trenches often gave away the soldiers' position, allowing intense fire to be directed at them with precision.

For a tommy in the trenches, a Pickelhaube, with its decorative front plate and spike, was a trophy worth having and Broughall was not going to be left out. Having stormed the German front line, he found himself in an enemy trench with one Captain Sadler, who recorded the incident for posterity. The captain had dispatched the remaining Germans in the dugout but Broughall, disappointed that they had all been wearing either steel helmets or foraging caps, announced he was after the finest Pickelhaube in the German army.

As reinforcements arrived, Broughall got his chance. Moving down the line, his men flushed out a rather large German sporting a fine spiked helmet and, rallying to his cry of 'Get that bloody hat,' his platoon gave chase. The German dashed up a communication trench but was eventually tackled to the ground, whereupon Broughall finally got his trophy. Unfortunately, in the general excitement, neither he nor his men had noticed that, in hot pursuit of their hat, they had now advanced past the second and third German lines and into the fourth line, which was still very much occupied by Germans.

Broughall's platoon mounted a heroic defence of the hat, however, and eventually this German line was taken too, the Pickelhaube having been responsible for one of the fastest, furthest and most successful advances of the day. It seemed almost a shame to tell Broughall that if he'd just waited a little longer in the front-line trench, he would have found hundreds of Pickelhauben.

How did democracy cause a disaster?

Few opponents proved more troublesome to the Roman republic than Hannibal and his Carthaginian army. The origins of the three Punic Wars between the states (of which Hannibal's campaign was the highlight of the second) are complicated, but they come down to a power struggle between two rising states over who should control the central Mediterranean. Considering the performance of the Roman command at Cannae, it's a miracle that it turned out to be a war they would win.

Since Hannibal had come over the Alps into Italy, the Roman army had already been brought to battle twice, at Trebbia and Lake Trasimeno, and they had lost very handsomely both times. Now, having made good their losses, the Romans decided to have another go and prepared to attack near Cannae. At this date Rome was a republic, its administration being run by annually elected magistrates who were drawn from the ruling class. These came in pairs, which was a useful balance in case one went off the rails a bit. And so it's no surprise to find that the Roman army massing at Cannae, all 87,000 of them, had two commanders rather than the usual one. So let's meet them.

First comes Lucius Aemilius Paullus, twice consul (top magistrate), father-in-law of the Carthaginian nemesis Scipio Africanus, victor of the Second Illyrian War and seasoned soldier. Then there was Gaius Terentius Varro, a career politician. As the Roman republic liked to divide things up equally, not only were there two commanders in charge of the legions but they took it in turns to take overall control – one day on, one day off. With two men as mismatched as Paullus and Varro, this would prove fatal.

At Cannae, the Romans managed to take the high ground overlooking the wide plain where Hannibal's forces were resting. For two weeks the two sides watched each other and for two weeks Varro tried to persuade Paullus to descend onto the plain and give battle. Paullus, a military man, was extremely reluctant to do this, as he would not only give away his main advantage but leave his infantry exposed to the numerous and well-trained Carthaginian cavalry. This clearly annoyed Varro but, thanks to the way the army was commanded, there was something he could do about it. As it happened, 1 August 216 BC was his day in charge and so, despite vehement protestations from Paullus, he marched the entire army from its commanding position down onto the plain. By the time this manouevre had been completed, it was too late to fight but it was also too late to go back. Varro went to bed, knowing that the following day his fellow commander would have to lead the Roman troops into battle and that, as it was his day off, he wouldn't have to organise it. Paullus, for his part, knew that he could not return to the heights as he'd expose the back of his army to the Carthaginians – so there was no choice but to fight.

The battle the following day, 2 August, proved extraordinary, even by the standards of the Second Punic War. The Roman army, having thrown away its major advantage, was brilliantly outflanked and annihilated. In a single day between 50,000 and 70,000 Roman troops were killed, making it one of the costliest battles of all time and possibly the greatest single loss of life in one engagement in one day ever. Lucius Aemilius Paullus died with his men in the general slaughter. Gaius Terentius Varro, who had got them into this situation but did not have to get them out of it, survived.

Who was Great Scott?

There is no conclusive proof as to who is being referred to in the phrase 'Great Scott' but the most likely candidate is a man known more usually as 'Old Fuss and Feathers'. Winfield Scott holds the record as the longest actively serving general in the US army, serving under fourteen administrations and in five major conflicts, as well as having an unsuccessful stab at becoming president himself.

His insistence on maintaining strict discipline and an exacting uniform code got him the title 'Old Fuss and Feathers' but it seems to have been an affectionate jibe. After the Mexican War he was a national hero and became the first American since George Washington to reach the rank of lieutenant general, a promotion granted by order of Congress. In the 1852 presidential election, the Whig Party nominated him as their candidate despite the fact that their own man, Millard Fillmore, was already president and rather hoped he might win another term. As it was, Scott's anti-slavery stance proved unpopular in the South and he lost in a landslide.

Revenge was not long in coming, however, and at the outbreak of the American Civil War, Scott – now weighing around twenty-one stone and too fat to ride a horse, let alone fight – is credited with devising a major part of the Union strategy for defeating the Confederacy in the civil war. It's from this period that newspapers start referring to 'Great Scott', a term that seems apposite both in terms of his size and reputation. Today Winfield Scott's reputation is not quite as spotless, mainly due to his role in the forced removal of the Cherokee Indians from their homelands along the 'Trail of Tears' in 1838, but his name at least lives on in the phrase.

How did a pilot postpone an invasion?

By 1649, with the English Civil War entering its endgame, most of the West Country had come under Parliamentarian control. The exception was one small group of islands lying some twenty miles west of Land's End in the Atlantic ocean – the Isles of Scilly.

Scilly had been staunchly Royalist and, in 1648, Sir John Grenville had been sent there by the king to organise the islands as a Royalist base, its distance from the mainland and its position in the shipping routes of the eastern approaches making it an ideal location. A year later the tide, as it were, had turned, transforming Scilly into an isolated outpost. Grenville had taken to raiding any passing shipping to replenish his stores (and line his pockets), making him a thorn in just about everyone's side, regardless of their political affiliation. The Parliamentarians finally decided to take action.

Robert Blake and his squadron of ships were dispatched to bring Grenville's raids to an end. In addition, their orders were to protect the Scillies from falling into the hands of the Dutch who, justly annoyed at having their ships seized and then sold back to them by the brazen Grenville, had taken to sending a fleet to patrol the area. Blake arrived off Scilly on 13 April 1649 and began preparing for his attack. Scouts and local spies told him that he should concentrate on taking the smaller islands of Tresco and Bryher, which commanded the main sea route through the islands but were less heavily defended than the largest island of St Mary's. Blake liked the idea as, with these islands in his hands, he could effectively control the port of St Mary's and cut off Grenville's supply lines. All he had to do now was take two very small islands.

The attack began on 17 April at 6 a.m. when forty boats set off from Blake's fleet in misty conditions to seize Tresco. Guiding them to their destination was a man called Nance, an inhabitant of the island who had been dragooned into their employment as a pilot and was apparently none too happy about it.

What happened next is somewhat confused, which is probably just how Nance liked it. Closing in on the fog-bound islands, the boats' crews became bewildered by all the small islets and rocks around them. Nance took advantage of their confusion to land three companies of men, not on Tresco but on the tiny uninhabited islet of Northwethel. The error was quickly spotted but the damage had been done. Whilst the men on Northwethel were re-embarked, the rest of the boats wallowed in the shallows off Tresco, some running aground, with the crew in others falling prey to seasickness. The element of surprise was lost and the Royalist garrison were alerted, mounting a determined fusillade from the beach. In the end only one of the boats managed to land on Tresco and that was forced quickly back, before the whole invasion was called off for the day.

Whether Nance had deliberately led the Parliamentarians astray remains a mystery. It would certainly be a bold move to lead so many armed men in the wrong direction single-handedly, and there's no evidence that the inhabitants of Scilly were particularly fond of the piratical Grenville, but then it is almost unheard of for a Scillonian to get his local navigation wrong. Nance may have simply been paying Blake back for having forced a Scillonian pilot into his service rather than paying him.

Who fought a civilised world war?

Even in the North African battlefields of the Second World War there was sometimes room for a little civilised behaviour, if the commanders of the respective forces were prepared to entertain such ideas. Fortunately for his opposite numbers, Hans von Luck was just such a man.

Hans-Ulrich von Luck und Witten came from an old Prussian military family that had served with Frederick the Great and could trace its roots back to the thirteenth century. After a classical education, he joined the army, first meeting his future mentor Erwin Rommel on a course in Dresden before being commissioned as a junior officer in the 1st Motorised battalion.

On the outbreak of the Second World War, von Luck saw action in most of the main theatres, serving in reconnaissance battalions during the invasions of Poland, France and the Soviet Union, but it was when reunited with Rommel in the Afrikakorps that von Luck lit upon the sort of war he had always wanted to fight. Following a temporary evacuation back to Germany to recuperate from a leg wound, von Luck returned to North Africa in September 1942 to command the 3rd Panzer Reconnaissance battalion of the 21st Panzer Division.

Von Luck believed war could and should be civilised, being fought under strict rules of gentlemanly behaviour. After a pleasant month playing cat and mouse with the British Long Range Desert group (the forerunner of the SAS), his hopes looked as though they might be dashed by the launch of Montgomery's Second Battle of El Alamein. Fortunately von Luck discovered that his opponents – the British Royal Dragoons – shared his views. Whilst the Afrikakorps desperately tried to hold their line as the Allied forces probed around their edges, hoping to outflank them, von Luck and the Dragoons fought a more orderly campaign. The two sides agreed that the war would stop at 5 p.m. each day for tea. Around 5.15 p.m. the German commander would ring his opposite number to enquire about the well-being of any of his men who had been captured and offer assurances of the good health of any prisoners he had taken that day.

A certain amount of 'trading' between the two sides also occurred with captured soldiers being 'ransomed' back in return for goods and supplies. When news reached von Luck that the British had received a supply of cigarettes, von Luck offered to trade the heir to the Players tobacco fortune, who was fortunately among his prisoners, in return for 1 million cigarettes for his men. The Dragoons countered with an offer of 600,000 and the deal was set to go ahead, until the Players heir, complaining that he was worth at least 1 million cigarettes, refused to be traded.

Von Luck survived the war and, after several years interned in a Russian gulag, returned to Germany, where he re-established his civilised links with his old enemy. In particular, he and Major John Howard, the British officer who led the assault on 'Pegasus' bridge during D-Day, would meet in the café in Caen that claimed to be the first building liberated from the Germans during Operation Overlord. Thus von Luck concluded his civilised war with a civilised peace.

How did Gustavus Adolphus say sorry?

Gustavus Adolphus, king of Sweden, was one of the great military commanders of the Thirty Years War, but his temper sometimes got him into trouble with some of his own more sensitive commanders.

One such tiff occurred during a review of troops at which the king reprimanded Colonel Seaton for some technical deficiencies in the parade. Seaton chose, perhaps unwisely, to answer back and the interview descended into pushing and shoving, during which the king slapped Seaton around the face.

Colonel Seaton was mortally offended. That evening, he went

to the royal apartments and demanded that the king sign his discharge papers. The monarch consented without another word, but he was already having second thoughts. Seaton was a very able commander and it was intolerable to learn that he was even then saddling up and making for Denmark to offer his services there.

So the following morning, Gustavus Adolphus and a handful of servants headed out after the piqued colonel, finally overtaking him at the Danish frontier. Here the king dismounted and made his apology in the way only a man known as 'The Lion of the North' could. Noting that they were both armed with pistols and swords, and both now outside the jurisdiction of Sweden – making them, in effect, equals – the king challenged his colonel to a duel.

Colonel Seaton was rather surprised by this turn of events – after all, it's not every day that a European sovereign challenges you to a duel. It also presented a number of knotty problems. It would be rude to refuse and might smack of cowardice, but if he accepted and then injured or killed the king, he would have a lot of explaining to do.

He therefore took the only course he could, and perhaps the one Gustavus Adolphus knew he must. Dismounting, he fell to his knees and, according to the *Percy Anecdotes*, announced: 'Sir, you have more than given me satisfaction, in condescending to make me your equal. God forbid that my sword should do any mischief to so brave and gracious a prince! Permit me to return to Stockholm; and allow me the honour to live and die in your service.'

And so the two men turned round and headed back to the capital, the spat in the parade ground now quite forgotten.

How did Philip of Macedon undermine his enemy?

Philip of Macedon, father of Alexander the Great, was himself a great military tactician and passed on to his son many of the mental skills that he would need to conquer much of the known world. Foremost among these was cheating.

When the game of war involves killing your enemy and taking their possessions, there seems little reason not to use every available trick and deceit. Philip was a master at this, which led to his appearing regularly in the military manuals of the ancient world. Frontinus, in his book *Strategems*, records a typical move.

Philip had attacked the city of Prinassus, which had proved a tough nut to crack. Having been thrown back from the walls, he had sacked the outlying houses and farms and then settled down to besieging the place. This usually meant bringing in miners to dig under the walls of the city, supporting their excavations on wooden props. Once the walls were thoroughly undermined, these props would be set on fire. Their collapse would bring the city walls tumbling into the caverns dug out beneath them and leave the besiegers free simply to walk into town.

This was the theory at Prinassus, but Philip's military engineers soon came across a difficulty. The walls of the town were not built on soil but on solid rock, which was impossible to dig through. This meant that they could not be undermined. A lesser commander might have given up at this point but not Philip. He knew that the walls were invulnerable but, he reasoned, did the Prinassians?

Taking a gamble that they didn't, he ordered his miners to dig short tunnels where they could and make a great deal of noise doing it, to convince the inhabitants that the mines were proceeding apace. Each night he sent men off to gather huge quantities of soil from elsewhere, which they piled around the excavations, suggesting that the hopeless mining was actually making massive headway. Philip then sent word to the Prinassians, warning them that he had undermined around 200 feet of their walls and was ready to fire the props. Thinking their walls were about to collapse, the people of Prinassus promptly surrendered.

What was glorious about the Glorious Revolution?

Revolutionary wars are really rather un-English, what with all that internecine fighting and bad feeling, so it is not surprising that when 'regime change' again came to the fore less than forty years after the English Civil War, the next revolution was, at least in England itself, a more civilised affair.

James II was not a universally popular king. The Whigs disliked his arbitrary suspension of parliamentary laws, whilst the Tories and the Church feared that his overt Catholicism threatened the established Protestant faith. As he was married to a Catholic queen who had given him a son and heir, a decidedly unwelcome, Catholic, autocratic future now seemed to stretch before many of his people. But how to get rid of him without starting a war?

The first thing was to find a suitable replacement, so the markedly Protestant William of Orange, James's nephew, was asked whether he'd care to take over. William willingly accepted, along with his wife Mary, who happened to be James's daughter and was hence second in line to the throne anyway. There was still the danger of conflict, however, and when, on 5 November 1688, the couple landed at Torbay, they took the precaution of bringing a Dutch army with them.

Fortunately this proved wholly unnecessary as, with William in the country, James II's own army refused to obey its Catholic officers. James had little option but to flee to France (taking the crown jewels with him). The parliament that sat on 22 January 1689 reasonably decided that James's flight across the Channel constituted an abdication, and asked William and Mary whether they would like to rule jointly. The succession would go to Mary's sister Anne if Mary were to have no children. It was further stipulated that Catholics were forbidden to sit on the throne; monarchs were no longer allowed to suspend laws; and a standing army was made illegal in peacetime. All this the happy couple accepted and so a very British revolution was concluded.

ACKNOWLEDGMENTS

This book is a collection of historical curiosities that I have gathered over the years as I went about writing books, making documentaries and advising on films. As such it includes the thoughts and suggestions of hundreds of people whom I've been fortunate enough to work with along the way. I hope you will forgive me if I don't list you all.

Writing stories is a pleasure but researching tales back to their source requires not only tenacity but a willingness to cast aside a wonderful anecdote when, after long pursuit, you find it to be nothing more than a house of cards. That has been the task that Stephanie, my wife, has undertaken on this book, following often tortuous paths back to obscure documents in the hope of finding a gem. If there are gems in these pages, they are hers and she is mine. It takes a rare historian to set out into the wilds of military history and come back still smiling.

For suggesting particular stories for this book I should add my special thanks to my father, Dr Matt Lee, Gordon Pollard, Stuart Hill, Paul Gott and Barrie Howe. Once again I am fortunate to have the best team in the business behind the book too – Roland Philipps, Rowan Yapp and Lucy Dixon at John Murray, my copy-editor Celia Levett, Julian Alexander at LAW and Richard Foreman at Chalke. It is also nothing short of a privilege to have my words illustrated by Martin Haake.

Finally, as always, I want to thank Connie, who is now old enough to read and will no doubt want to see her name in this as in all my previous books. The notes and treasures she leaves on my desk are as much an inspiration to me as the stories of philosophers and kings.

INDEX